Cornelia Schinharl

NOODLES

A VEGETARIAN JOURNEY
THROUGH THE WORLD OF PASTA

PHOTOGRAPHY
Heinz-Josef Beckers

Translated from the German by Helen Feingold

BARRON'S

TABLE OF CONTENTS

For All Tastes

Wherever you live, whether you call them noodles or pasta, these simple mixtures of flour, salt, oil, and eggs and/or water form the backbone of many of the world's cuisines.

Whether noodles were placed on tables first in China or Italy, were created at almost the same time on both continents, or were already loved by the Etruscans, one thing is certain: Even today, Italians and Asians have the largest repertoire of noodle dishes.

Many an Italian family wouldn't think of passing a day without pasta, mostly served as the main dish but also as an appetizer or side dish. In Asia, noodles are served in soup or out of the wok. In China, long noodles symbolize a long life, and for this reason they are most important at a birthday party.

Noodles – Nearly the quickest dish in the world

Can you think of any other preparation that requires so little time and effort as a plate of steaming spaghetti? If you have very little time for shopping and cooking or unexpected guests are standing at your door, you hold the trump card with pasta. It's even tasty tossed with just garlic and good olive oil, and every good cook surely has these ingredients on hand.

Shopping for the Best

The list of pasta or noodle varieties is endless; the folded front cover shows only a small selection. The quality of pasta you buy determines just how good the meal will finally be. The simpler the sauce, the more important it is to buy the highest quality pasta.

Good Italian pastas are made of hard wheat flour (durum semolina) to achieve the desired consistency. When made with only water and salt, they are called in Italian *pasta secca*. Spaghetti, penne, farfalle and most other Italian pastas belong in this group. Packages are always labeled if the product is made with egg (*pasta all'uovo*). Years ago in Italy, noodles made with egg were prepared only for special feast days.

Asian noodles are made with or without eggs, using wheat, buckwheat, or rice flour, or mung bean starch (transparent noodles). Most are sold dried, but now many supermarkets sell them fresh in vacuum packs.

Perfect Storage

Dried noodles can be stored for a year if the opened packages are kept in airtight jars. Fill several different jars with a variety of noodles for a decorative display on the kitchen counter. Fresh noodles, whether Italian or homemade, cannot be stored without drying and are best when used within two to three days of preparation. To store, dry noodles thoroughly on kitchen towels, turning several times. Transfer to glass jars and seal. Fresh noodles can also be frozen on cookie sheets. When hard, seal them in freezer containers. To store homemade stuffed pastas, freeze them in a single layer on a cookie sheet, then wrap and store in the freezer. To cook, drop them still frozen into boiling salted water. They need only 1 to 2 minutes longer to cook than when fresh, and they taste just as good.

Important Staples

With these items in your refrigerator and pantry, you have the basics:

Assorted noodle shapes—
2 packages of each variety
A few cans of peeled tomatoes
1 jar capers
1 can black olives
1 jar dried tomatoes packed in oil
1 jar pesto
1 piece Parmesan or Pecorino cheese
Dried or frozen herbs
Garlic
Cold-pressed olive oil

Oven Temperature

Both gas and electric ovens must be preheated to the temperature required in the recipe. Occasionally check oven temperature with an oven thermometer to make sure the thermostat is accurate.

cold
&
hot

Salads and Soups

Who says pasta must always come to the table topped with sauce? Noodles are irresistible when made into a salad with a good dressing or ladled out of a steaming soup pot. Both salads and soups can be prepared ahead of time for parties and are suitable for large groups.

Noodles soften a bit when mixed with moist dressings and are allowed to stand. Therefore, it is important not to overcook noodles for salad. In contrast to pasta served hot, noodles for salad should be rinsed with cold water; this stops the cooking at once and washes off surface starch to keep the noodles from sticking together.

You can prepare salads for parties in double, triple, or quadruple portions in the morning, cover with foil, and store in the refrigerator.

For the office

Here's a delicious lunch for 1 person. The night before, cook 2½ oz (60–70 g) noodles and rinse with cold water. Drain. Prepare a dressing by mixing 2 oz (50 g) diced cheese (mozzarella, blue cheese, or Swiss), 1 diced tomato, 2 to 3 olives cut into strips, and the shredded leaves of ½ bunch fresh basil. Stir in ¼ teaspoon prepared mustard, 1½ teaspoons vinegar or lemon juice, and 1 tablespoon oil. Fold in noodles and season to taste with salt and pepper. Spoon into a plastic tub with a tight-fitting lid and chill overnight. Before eating, stir lightly to blend.

Vegetable Broth (Basic Recipe)

Soups taste the very best when prepared with homemade broths. Vegetarians can cook a well-seasoned broth of vegetables and herbs: 2¼ to 4½ lbs (1–2 kg) mixed vegetables (carrots, fennel, leeks, tomatoes, celery) washed, peeled, and diced. Put vegetables in a stockpot and add 1 halved onion, 2 peeled garlic cloves, and 2 bay leaves. Add 1 bunch mixed fresh herbs and, if desired, 1 dried chili pepper. Add 1½ qts (1.5 l) water, cover, and bring to boil. Add salt, cover, and cook over moderate heat 30 minutes. Cool and then strain, pressing to squeeze out all broth. Season to taste.

When you prepare your own vegetable broth, you have the luxury of producing large quantities that can be frozen for future use. This makes it even easier to make a tasty soup.

Asian Seasoning

Noodle soup from the Far East tastes best with a light broth seasoned with rice vinegar, a little sugar or honey, sambal oelek (a condiment made up of chiles, brown sugar, and salt), crumbled dried chilies or chili oil, salt, and soy sauce. During the cooking, add a walnut-size piece of peeled and thinly sliced fresh ginger root to the pot.

Soup for a Crowd

When you prepare soup for a large group and it must keep hot for a long time, cook the noodles separately. Rinse with cold water and drain well. Place them in a large bowl near the soup pot. Each guest can fill his bowl with noodles and then ladle boiling hot soup over them. They will quickly warm and won't fall apart as they would if kept in the hot soup for a long time.

Quickest of All Dressings

With a few diced tomatoes or cucumbers and a well-seasoned vinaigrette, noodle leftovers taste as good the next day as they did freshly cooked.

Vinaigrette

Mix 1 shallot or small red onion, finely chopped, with 1 teaspoon sharp Dijon or grain mustard, and 1½ tablespoons white wine vinegar or lemon juice. Beat in 3 tablespoons oil and season to taste with salt and pepper. Stir in chopped fresh herbs to taste.

Cheese Dressing

Beat 2 oz (50 g) ricotta or blue cheese with 2 tablespoons heavy cream and 2 tablespoons oil. Season to taste with lemon juice and desired seasonings.

Fusilli Salad with Lentils
½ cup (100 g) lentils
Salt
8 oz (200 g) fusilli
1 bunch green onions
4 young carrots
1 red bell pepper
1 bunch chives
*1 tablespoon red wine
vinegar*
*2 tablespoons balsamic
vinegar*
Black pepper
½ teaspoon hot paprika
¼ cup (60 ml) olive oil
*4 teaspoons crème fraîche
(or sour cream)*

*Preparation time: 30 to
40 minutes*

Penne Salad with Avocado Cream
Salt
*9 oz (250 g) penne or elbow
macaroni*
1½ lbs (600 g) tomatoes
1 bunch green onions
*2 sprigs lemon balm or
parsley*
1 ripe avocado
2 tablespoons lemon juice
1 garlic clove, pressed
*1 teaspoon sharp prepared
mustard*
½ cup (125 ml) buttermilk
Cayenne pepper

*Preparation time: about
30 minutes*

Fusilli Salad with Lentils

Pictured • Economical

• Cover lentils with plenty of water, bring to boil, cover, and cook over medium heat 25 to 35 minutes or until tender but not mushy.

• For fusilli, bring plenty of water to boil. Add salt and fusilli and cook according to package directions until tender but still firm (al dente). Rinse with cold water and drain.

• Clean green onions, wash, and chop finely. Peel carrots and cut into thin strips. Clean pepper and cut into thin strips. Cut chives into thin rings.

• Mix vinegars with salt, pepper, and paprika. Whisk in oil. Drain lentils and mix with fusilli, vegetables, and dressing. Season and spoon onto plates. Serve garnished with a teaspoon of crème fraîche.

Makes 4 servings.

PER SERVING:	351 CALORIES	
NUTRITIONAL INFORMATION		
Fat (24% calories from fat) 10	g
Protein 14	g
Carbohydrate 54	g
Cholesterol 53	mg
Sodium 1	mg

Penne Salad with Avocado Cream

Summer dish • Economical

• For penne, bring plenty of water to boil. Add salt and penne and boil until tender but still firm (al dente). Drain, rinse with cold water, and drain again.

• Core tomatoes and cut into small cubes. Trim green onions and cut into thin rings. Cut herb leaves into strips.

• For avocado cream, halve avocado and remove pit. Scoop flesh from skin and mash smoothly. Mix puree with lemon juice. Stir in garlic, mustard, and buttermilk. Season with salt and cayenne.

• Lightly mix penne with tomatoes, green onions, lemon balm, and avocado cream. Arrange on lettuce leaves.

Makes 4 servings.

PER SERVING:	331 CALORIES	
NUTRITIONAL INFORMATION		
Fat (26% calories from fat) 10	g
Protein 14	g
Carbohydrate 50	g
Cholesterol 3	mg
Sodium 34	mg

Orecchiette Salad with Almond Cream

Orecchiette Salad with Almond Cream
Salt
9 oz (250 g) orecchiette
1 young zucchini
4 oz (100 g) tender young spinach
2 bunches fresh basil
9 oz (250 g) ripe tomatoes
2 garlic cloves, peeled
4 oz (100 g) blanched almonds
1 tablespoon olive oil
Black pepper

Preparation time: about 25 minutes

Colorful Fusilli Salad with Cheese
Salt
9 oz (250 g) fusilli or penne
1 small cucumber
1 bunch watercress
1 bunch radishes
5 oz (150 g) Swiss cheese
6 tablespoons sour cream
1 tablespoon olive oil
1 tablespoon lemon juice
Black pepper
2 tablespoons sunflower seeds

Preparation time: about 20 minutes

Orecchiette Salad with Almond Cream

Elegant • Pictured

• For orecchiette, bring plenty of water to boil. Add salt and orecchiette and boil until tender but still firm (al dente). Rinse with cold water and drain.

• Cut zucchini into julienne strips. Trim spinach and wash well to remove sand. Drain well and tear leaves into large pieces. Set aside a few basil leaves and cut remaining leaves into thin strips.

• Core tomatoes and dip into boiling water for a few seconds. Peel off skins and cut tomatoes into large pieces.

• Combine garlic and almonds in food processor and chop finely. Transfer to large bowl and stir in tomatoes and oil. Fold in orecchiette, vegetables, and basil strips. Season to taste with salt and pepper. Garnish with reserved basil leaves.

Makes 4 servings.

Colorful Fusilli Salad with Cheese

Economical • Quick

• For fusilli, bring plenty of water to boil. Add salt and fusilli and boil until tender but still firm (al dente). Rinse with cold water and drain well.

• Trim cucumber and cut into small cubes. Pick over watercress and pull off leaves. Slice radishes; halve slices. Cut cheese into small cubes.

• Mix sour cream with oil and lemon juice. Mix with fusilli, cucumber, watercress, radishes, and cheese. Season with salt and pepper. Place salad in bowl.

• Toast sunflower seeds in dry skillet over medium heat, stirring constantly, until golden and fragrant. Sprinkle over salad.

Makes 4 servings.

PER SERVING:	405 CALORIES	
NUTRITIONAL INFORMATION		
Fat (39% calories from fat) 18	g
Protein 15	g
Carbohydrate 48	g
Cholesterol 59	mg
Sodium 7	mg

PER SERVING:	439 CALORIES	
NUTRITIONAL INFORMATION		
Fat (39% calories from fat) 19	g
Protein 23	g
Carbohydrate 44	g
Cholesterol 29	mg
Sodium 0	mg

Noodle Salad with Sugar-Snap or Snow Peas

Easy to prepare • Elegant

• For noodles, bring plenty of water to boil. Add salt and noodles and boil until tender but still firm (al dente). Drain, rinse with cold water, and drain again.

• Trim peas and blanch in boiling salted water about 3 minutes. Rinse with cold water and drain.

• Trim greens, wash thoroughly, and shred leaves.

• In a bowl, whisk egg yolks with mustard and 1 tablespoon lemon juice. Whisk in oil drop by drop until thick mayonnaise forms.

• Stir sour cream and lemon peel into mayonnaise. Stir in a little lemon juice. Season with salt and cayenne.

• Mix noodles with peas, greens, and mayonnaise. Season with salt.

• Toast pine nuts in dry pan over medium heat, stirring constantly, until golden. Sprinkle over salad and serve.

Makes 4 servings.

Variation:

Substitute alfalfa or clover sprouts for greens.

Tip

You can also prepare mayonnaise with cooked egg yolks. Hard-cook 3 eggs in simmering water about 8 minutes. Drain and rinse with cold water. Shell. Remove yolks and mash. Add 2 teaspoons mustard, 2 teaspoons lemon juice, and 2 tablespoons hot water and beat to blend. Gradually beat in ½ cup (125 ml) oil. Season to taste.

Salt
9 oz (250 g) wide noodles
9 oz (250 g) sugar-snap or snow peas
5 oz (150 g) dandelion greens, arugula, or watercress
2 egg yolks
1 teaspoon sharp mustard
Juice and grated peel of ½ lemon
½ cup (125 ml) olive oil
½ cup (125 g) sour cream
Cayenne pepper
2 tablespoons pine nuts

Preparation time: about 35 minutes

PER SERVING:	486 CALORIES	
NUTRITIONAL INFORMATION		
Fat (41% calories from fat) 22		g
Protein 14		g
Carbohydrate 58		g
Cholesterol 165		mg
Sodium 152		mg

Rice Noodle Salad with Cilantro

Elegant • Easy to prepare

• Cook rice noodles in boiling salted water 3 to 4 minutes or until tender but still firm. Add bean sprouts and bring to boil. Rinse with cold water and drain.

• Peel daikon and cut into thin strips. Halve pepper, clean, and cut into thin strips.

• Coarsely chop garlic. Remove core and seeds from chili. Pull off leaves from cilantro.

• In food processor, puree garlic, chili, cilantro, saté, lime juice, rice wine, and soy sauce. Thin with 1 to 2 tablespoons water. Season with salt.

• Mix rice noodles with sprouts, daikon, and red pepper and place on plates. Drizzle with sauce and serve garnished with cilantro leaves.

Makes 4 servings.

PER SERVING:	228 CALORIES
NUTRITIONAL INFORMATION	
Fat (3% calories from fat) 1	g
Protein 3	g
Carbohydrate 51	g
Cholesterol 0	mg
Sodium 1037	mg

Transparent Noodles with Spicy Carrots

Economical • Pictured

• Soak transparent noodles in lukewarm water 30 minutes. Soak mushrooms in water.

• Wash chives and cut into ½-in (1 cm) pieces. Toast cashews until golden.

• Peel ginger and garlic and mince. Peel carrots and cut into julienne strips. Drain mushrooms and cut out hard stems.

• Heat oil in large skillet and sauté carrots 3 minutes. Add garlic, ginger, and mushroom caps and sauté 1 minute. Stir in ¼ cup (60 ml) water, lemon juice, sambal oelek, and honey. Season with salt.

• Drain transparent noodles. Add to skillet and sauté briefly. Stir in chives and cashews. Cool, then chill.

Makes 4 servings.

PER SERVING:	281 CALORIES
NUTRITIONAL INFORMATION	
Fat (31% calories from fat) 10	g
Protein 3	g
Carbohydrate 46	g
Cholesterol 0	mg
Sodium 15	mg

Rice Noodle Salad with Cilantro

8 oz (200 g) wide rice noodles
Salt
2 oz (50 g) mung bean sprouts
1 small daikon (Oriental white radish)
1 red bell pepper
2 garlic cloves
1 red chili pepper
10 to 12 sprigs fresh cilantro (coriander)
3 tablespoons saté sauce (sold in Asian markets)
2 to 3 tablespoons lime juice
3 tablespoons rice wine (or water)
3 tablespoons light soy sauce
Fresh cilantro leaves for garnish

Preparation time: about 25 minutes

Transparent Noodles with Carrots

5 oz (150 g) transparent or cellophane noodles
15 small dried shiitake mushrooms
1 bunch chives
3 tablespoons chopped cashews
Walnut-size piece fresh ginger root
3 garlic cloves
1 lb (450 g) young carrots
2 tablespoons peanut oil
Juice and grated peel of ½ lemon
1½ teaspoons sambal oelek (sold in Asian markets)
1½ teaspoons honey
Salt

Preparation time: about 40 minutes

Yogurt Soup with Orzo

Economical • Elegant

• Finely chop onion. Melt butter in soup pot and sauté onion until translucent.

• Add broth and bring to boil. Add orzo and cook, covered, over medium heat 8 to 10 minutes or until tender but still firm (al dente).

• Whisk yogurt with eggs and flour. Cut mint leaves into strips.

• Remove soup from heat. Mix yogurt mixture with 1 soup ladle of hot broth, then mix this into remaining broth.

• Warm soup over low heat, stirring constantly, until thickened; do not allow to boil.

• Season soup with lemon juice, salt, pepper, and paprika. Serve soup sprinkled with mint.

Makes 4 servings.

PER SERVING:		380 CALORIES
NUTRITIONAL INFORMATION		
Fat (30% calories from fat) 13	g	
Protein 15	g	
Carbohydrate 52	g	
Cholesterol 174	mg	
Sodium 1748	mg	

Penne Soup with Feta Cheese

Pictured • Quick

• Clean green onions and cut with tender greens into thin rings. Cut zucchini into sticks ½-in (1 cm) wide.

• Heat oil in skillet and sauté zucchini over medium heat 4 to 5 minutes or until golden brown. Press garlic over zucchini. Season with salt and pepper.

• Bring vegetable broth to boil. Add penne and cook until tender but still firm (al dente).

• Finely chop herbs. Crumble feta cheese.

• Stir zucchini and green onions into soup and reheat. Season with salt and pepper. Ladle into soup bowls and sprinkle with herbs and cheese.

Makes 4 servings.

PER SERVING:		496 CALORIES
NUTRITIONAL INFORMATION		
Fat (30% calories from fat) 17	g	
Protein 22	g	
Carbohydrate 67	g	
Cholesterol 64	mg	
Sodium 1749	mg	

Yogurt Soup with Orzo
1 onion
1 tablespoon butter
1 qt (1 l) vegetable broth
4 oz (100 g) orzo (pasta shaped like rice grains)
1½ cups (300 g) plain yogurt
2 small eggs
1 tablespoon all-purpose flour
2 sprigs fresh mint
1 to 2 tablespoons lemon juice
Salt
Black pepper
½ teaspoon hot paprika

Preparation time: about 20 minutes

Penne Soup with Feta Cheese
1 bunch green onions
10 oz (300 g) young zucchini
2 garlic cloves
2 tablespoons olive oil
Salt and black pepper
1 qt (1 l) vegetable broth
8 oz (200 g) penne (or fusilli)
4 to 5 sprigs lemon balm
½ bunch parsley
5 oz (150 g) Feta cheese

Preparation time: about 30 minutes

Tomato Soup

1¾ lbs (750 g) tomatoes
1 shallot
2 garlic cloves
1 bunch fresh basil
1 tablespoon olive oil
Salt and black pepper
Cayenne pepper
¼ teaspoon (1 ml) honey
5 oz (150 g) spinach noodles
5 oz (150 g) Gorgonzola
cheese
1 tablespoon pine nuts

Preparation time: about
35 minutes

Asian Noodle Soup

9 oz (250 g) tofu
1 walnut-size piece fresh
ginger root
2 garlic cloves
1 teaspoon ground cumin
1 tablespoon lemon juice
Salt
1 bunch green onions
4 oz (100 g) cherry tomatoes
1 bunch fresh basil
1 qt (1 l) vegetable broth
5 oz (150 g) Chinese egg
noodles
1 to 2 tablespoons rice
vinegar
1 to 2 teaspoons honey
Few drops chili oil

Preparation time: about
45 minutes

20

Tomato Soup with Spinach Noodles

Pictured • Elegant

• Core tomatoes. Dip into boiling water a few seconds and skin. Cut into small cubes. Mince shallot and garlic. Set aside a few tender basil leaves and finely chop remaining basil.

• Heat oil in soup pot. Sauté shallot, garlic, and chopped basil until wilted. Add tomatoes and sauté briefly. Add 2 cups (500 ml) water and bring to boil. Season with salt, pepper, cayenne, and honey. Cover and simmer about 10 minutes.

• For noodles, bring plenty of water to boil. Break noodles into pieces. Add salt and noodles to water and boil until tender but still firm.

• Dice cheese. Drain noodles. Stir noodles and cheese into soup.

• Toast pine nuts until golden. Sprinkle each serving with pine nuts and reserved basil leaves.

Makes 4 servings.

PER SERVING:	345 CALORIES	
NUTRITIONAL INFORMATION		
Fat (44% calories from fat)	17	g
Protein	15	g
Carbohydrate	33	g
Cholesterol	36	mg
Sodium	44	mg

Asian Noodle Soup with Tofu

Low in calories • Light

• Drain tofu and cut into ½-in (1 cm) cubes. Coarsely chop ginger and garlic. Force both through a press. Add them to tofu with cumin, lemon juice, and salt. Let marinate 30 minutes.

• Clean green onions and cut with tender greens into thin rings. Halve cherry tomatoes. Cut basil leaves into strips.

• Heat vegetable broth. Add noodles and cook until tender but still firm (al dente).

• Stir in green onions, tofu mixture, cherry tomatoes, and basil. Reheat.

• Season with rice vinegar, honey, chili oil, and salt. Serve at once.

Makes 4 servings.

PER SERVING:	385 CALORIES	
NUTRITIONAL INFORMATION		
Fat (19% calories from fat)	9	g
Protein	18	g
Carbohydrate	63	g
Cholesterol	3	mg
Sodium	2047	mg

Broth with Chickpeas and Cheese Ravioli

Elegant • Easy to prepare

• For dough, mix flour with eggs, oil, and 1 teaspoon salt. Knead into smooth, elastic dough on floured surface (see page 50). If dough is dry, mix in a little water; if sticky, knead in more flour. Roll dough into ball, cover, and let rest at room temperature about 30 minutes.

• For filling, finely dice fontina and Gorgonzola and mix with Parmesan. Finely chop basil leaves. Peel garlic and force through press. Add both to cheeses. Season lightly with salt (cheese is already salty) and cayenne.

• Knead dough again, divide in half and roll each piece into thin sheet on floured surface. Place teaspoons of filling in mounds 1½ in (2–3 cm) apart on one sheet of dough. Brush dough between mounds with water. Cover with second sheet of dough and press dough firmly together between mounds of filling. Cut into ravioli with pastry wheel or sharp knife. Dip tines of a fork into flour and firmly press edges together. Place ravioli side by side on kitchen towel.

• For soup, trim spinach and wash thoroughly several times in cold water. Drain. Cut carrots into julienne strips.

• For ravioli, bring plenty of salted water to boil. Boil ravioli 3 minutes or until tender but still firm (al dente). Bring vegetable broth to boil. Add spinach, carrots, and chickpeas and simmer 3 minutes.

• Season soup with salt and pepper. Drain ravioli and spoon into serving bowls. Ladle soup into bowls. Serve garnished with chives.

Makes 4 servings.

For ravioli:
1⅓ cups (200 g) all-purpose flour
2 eggs
1 teaspoon olive oil
Salt
Flour for work surface

For filling:
4 oz (100 g) fontina cheese
4 oz (100 g) Gorgonzola cheese
2 oz (50 g) Parmesan cheese, freshly grated
1 bunch fresh basil
2 garlic cloves
Salt
Cayenne pepper

For soup:
10 oz (300 g) spinach leaves
1 small carrot
1 qt (1 l) vegetable broth
1 can (15 oz/400 g) chickpeas, drained
Salt
Black pepper
2 tablespoons chopped chives

Preparation time: about 1½ hours

PER SERVING:	767 CALORIES	
NUTRITIONAL INFORMATION		
Fat (34% calories from fat) 29		g
Protein 39		g
Carbohydrate 89		g
Cholesterol 195		mg
Sodium .2293		mg

With sauce, please!

Quick Noodle Dishes

How many foods are as easy and appealing as noodles?

There are a thousand and one shapes available, bringing endless variations to the table. If you're careful with cooking, the results are guaranteed.

Use plenty of water; for 4 oz (100 g) noodles, pour 1 qt (1 l) water into a large (at least 6 qt/6 l) pot and bring to boil.

For each quart (liter), add 1 heaping teaspoon salt, preferably sea salt. Oil is not necessary in the cooking water.

Push long noodles carefully into the boiling water with a large cooking spoon as soon as the ends soften. Cook uncovered, timing the cooking from when the water returns to a boil.

After a few minutes, stir carefully with a wooden spoon to keep noodles from sticking to the bottom of the pot. Stir several times during cooking.

Cooking times

Perfectly cooked noodles are not hard and white in the center, but tender yet still firm. In Italian, this is called "al dente," meaning "to the tooth." The pasta feels a little resistant to the teeth when chewed.

Most packages give a suggested cooking time, but test noodles often to keep them from getting too soft. As a rule, most noodles need about 8 minutes from the time the water returns to a boil. Thicker noodles like orecchiette, conchiglione, and macaroni often need up to 13 minutes. After cooking, noodles (other than those for salad) should not be rinsed. To keep them from cooling, drain them in a colander and quickly mix noodles with hot sauce or 1 to 2 tablespoons olive oil in a warmed bowl. In this way, noodles will not stick together. Also, drain noodles thoroughly if they are to be mixed with a thin sauce. Noodles that are mixed with a thick sauce or with smaller amounts of sauce should be drained quickly to keep them moist and to prevent the pasta dish from being too dry.

Classic Italian Pasta Dishes

Here is a short list of the best noodle sauces.

• Tomato Sauce

Finely chop 1 onion, 2 garlic cloves, 1 small carrot, 1 celery stalk. Sauté in 2 tablespoons olive oil. Add 2 lbs (800 g) peeled and diced tomatoes with 2 teaspoons chopped fresh rosemary. Season with salt and pepper and cook uncovered, stirring occasionally, 30 to 60 minutes or until sauce is thick. At this time, season again and stir in finely chopped fresh basil to taste.

• Pesto

In a food processor, coarsely puree leaves of 4 bunches fresh basil, 2 peeled garlic cloves and 4 oz (100 g) pine nuts. Add 2 oz (50 g) grated pecorino cheese. While processor is running, slowly add ½ cup (100 ml) olive oil. Season with salt and papper. Can be frozen.

• Spicy Garlic Oil *(Aglio e Olio)*

Finely chop 3 peeled garlic cloves and 1 to 2 dried chili peppers. Chop ½ bunch parsley. Heat 7 to 8 tablespoons olive oil and sauté garlic, chilies, and parsley briefly. Mix with quickly drained spaghetti. Serve with grated cheese.

Many pasta dishes are incomplete without grated cheese.

Parmesan comes from Parma in Emilia Romagna. It is made from cow's milk and must ripen at least 18 months before it can be stamped (branded) and sold.

A little spicy, with shorter ripening time, is grana Padana.

Spicy and mostly made from sheep's milk, harder pecorino is good for grating.

Note: Always grate cheeses fresh; do not buy packaged grated cheese.

Grated Cheeses

Parmesan and pecorino are classic toppings for many Italian pasta dishes. For full enjoyment, always grate cheese right at the table and sprinkle directly on pasta. For this purpose, a piece of cheese can be put into a hand grater and placed on the table ready to be grated directly over each serving.

Penne with Tomato Ricotta Sauce

1½ lbs (600 g) tomatoes
1 red onion
2 garlic cloves
2 to 3 sprigs fresh rosemary
1 tablespoon olive oil
Salt
Black pepper
1 lb (400 g) penne
4 oz (100 g) ricotta or
cottage cheese
Freshly grated Parmesan for
topping

Preparation time: about
35 minutes

Tagliatelle, Mushrooms, and Tomatoes

½ oz (10 g) dried Italian
mushrooms
4 oz (100 g) dried tomatoes,
packed in oil
Salt
1 lb (400 g) tagliatelle
1 tablespoon capers
1 large bunch parsley
1 garlic clove
2 tablespoons olive oil
2 tablespoons pine nuts
Black pepper

Preparation time: about
25 minutes

Penne with Tomato Ricotta Sauce

Pictured • Economical

• Core tomatoes. Dip briefly into boiling water and peel. Halve and finely dice. Finely chop onion and garlic. Chop rosemary.

• Heat oil in pot. Sauté onion, garlic, and rosemary until onion is translucent. Add tomatoes, salt, and pepper and cook uncovered over medium heat 10 minutes or until thickened.

• For penne, bring plenty of water to boil. Add salt and cook penne until al dente.

• Spoon ricotta into tomato sauce. Drain penne and mix lightly with sauce. Spoon onto warmed plates. Serve with Parmesan.

Makes 4 servings.

Variation:

For a spicier sauce, cook 1 to 2 dried chili peppers with tomatoes.

PER SERVING:	468 CALORIES	
NUTRITIONAL INFORMATION		
Fat (19% calories from fat) 10		g
Protein 22		g
Carbohydrate 73		g
Cholesterol 15		mg
Sodium 36		mg

Tagliatelle, Mushrooms, and Tomatoes

Elegant • Quick

• Soak mushrooms in lukewarm water about 15 minutes. Drain well and chop finely. Finely chop tomatoes.

• For tagliatelle, bring plenty of water to boil. Add salt and tagliatelle and cook until al dente.

• Drain capers and chop coarsely. Finely chop parsley leaves and garlic.

• Heat oil in pot and sauté pine nuts with mushrooms. Add tomatoes, capers, garlic, and parsley and stir a few minutes.

• Drain tagliatelle and stir into tomato mixture. Season with salt and pepper. Serve at once on warmed plates.

Makes 4 servings.

PER SERVING:	515 CALORIES	
NUTRITIONAL INFORMATION		
Fat (17% calories from fat) 10		g
Protein 17		g
Carbohydrate 92		g
Cholesterol 0		mg
Sodium 550		mg

Spaghetti with Four-Cheese Sauce

Quick • Pictured

• Clean green onions. Finely chop 2 of the green onions and their tender greens. Cut remaining green onions into thin rings, cover, and set aside. Seed and finely chop red pepper. Finely grate pecorino and cut other cheeses into very small cubes.

• For spaghetti, bring plenty of water to boil. Add salt and spaghetti and boil until al dente.

• Heat oil in pot. Sauté chopped green onions and chili pepper until wilted. Add vegetable broth and heat. Stir in cheeses, wine, and lemon juice to taste. Cook over low heat, stirring, until thick. Season with salt and pepper.

• Drain spaghetti and mix with cheese sauce. Serve sprinkled with green onion rings.

Makes 4 servings.

Penne with Gorgonzola

Rich • Easy

• For penne, bring plenty of water to boil. Add salt and penne and boil until al dente. Reserve ¼ cup (50 ml) cooking water.

• Halve, clean, and finely dice peppers. Peel garlic. Dice Gorgonzola. Toast pine nuts in dry skillet over low heat until golden.

• Heat oil in pot and sauté peppers over medium heat about 2 minutes.

• Add cream, Gorgonzola, and reserved penne cooking water and heat. Stir sauce over low heat until cheese is melted. Press garlic into sauce. Season with salt and pepper.

• Mix penne with sauce. Serve on warmed plates sprinkled with pine nuts.

Makes 4 servings.

Spaghetti with Four-Cheese Sauce
4 green onions
1 piece red chili pepper
2 oz (50 g) pecorino
2 oz (50 g) fontina
2 oz (50 g) Gorgonzola
2 oz (50 g) mozzarella
Salt
1 lb (400 g) spaghetti
1½ teaspoons olive oil
1 cup (250 ml) vegetable broth
2 tablespoons dry white wine
Lemon juice
Black pepper

Preparation time: about 25 minutes

Penne with Gorgonzola
Salt
1 lb (400 g) penne
1 lb (400 g) mixed red and yellow bell peppers
1 garlic clove
5 oz (150 g) Gorgonzola
1 tablespoon pine nuts
1 tablespoon olive oil
½ cup (100 ml) heavy cream
Black pepper

Preparation time: about 25 minutes

PER SERVING:	621 CALORIES	
NUTRITIONAL INFORMATION		
Fat (27% calories from fat)	19	g
Protein	28	g
Carbohydrate	88	g
Cholesterol	21	mg
Sodium	538	mg

PER SERVING:	614 CALORIES	
NUTRITIONAL INFORMATION		
Fat (37% calories from fat)	26	g
Protein	22	g
Carbohydrate	77	g
Cholesterol	121	mg
Sodium	2	mg

Tagliatelle with Poppy Seed Butter

1 lb (400 g) young carrots
Salt
1 lb (400 g) tagliatelle
½ bunch parsley
1 heaping tablespoon butter
3 tablespoons poppy seeds
Black pepper

Preparation time: about 25 minutes

Fettuccine with Leek Sauce

1¼ lbs (500 g) young leeks
1 garlic clove
Salt
1 lb (400 g) fettuccine
1½ oz (40 g) sliced almonds
1 tablespoon butter
Black pepper
½ cup (125 ml) heavy cream
1 handful fresh chervil

Preparation time: about 30 minutes

Tagliatelle with Poppy Seed Butter
Elegant • Pictured

• Trim and peel carrots. Cut into 2-in (5 cm) pieces, then into ¼-in (3 mm) sticks. Blanch carrots in boiling water 3 to 4 minutes. Rinse with cold water and drain well.

• For tagliatelle, bring plenty of water to boil. Add salt and tagliatelle and boil until al dente.

• Finely chop parsley leaves. Melt butter in medium pan. Add poppy seeds and sauté over medium heat about 1 minute. Add carrots and parsley and heat. Season with salt and pepper.

• Drain tagliatelle lightly to keep pasta moist. Stir in carrot mixture. Serve on warmed plates.

Makes 4 servings.

Fettuccine with Leek Sauce
Economical • Quick

• Trim and wash leeks. Cut into thin strips. Chop garlic.

• For fettuccine, bring plenty of water to boil. Add salt and fettuccine and boil until al dente. Reserve ⅓ cup (75 ml) cooking water.

• Toast almonds in dry skillet over medium heat, stirring, until golden.

• Melt butter in pan and sauté leeks and garlic until translucent. Add reserved fettuccine cooking water and season with salt and pepper. Cover and cook over low heat 5 minutes. Stir in cream and almonds. Bring sauce to boil. Tear off chervil leaves and set some aside for garnish. Drain fettuccine and mix with sauce and chervil. Serve garnished with reserved chervil.

Makes 4 servings.

PER SERVING:	445 CALORIES
NUTRITIONAL INFORMATION	

Fat (13% calories from fat)	6	g
Protein	15	g
Carbohydrate	80	g
Cholesterol	8	mg
Sodium	7	mg

PER SERVING:	569 CALORIES
NUTRITIONAL INFORMATION	

Fat (26% calories from fat)	16	g
Protein	21	g
Carbohydrate	84	g
Cholesterol	42	mg
Sodium	10	mg

Rigatoni with Red Vegetable Cream

Pictured • Easy to prepare

• Cook beets, covered, in enough water to cover generously, over medium heat until tender, about 40 to 50 minutes. Rinse with cold water, peel, and chop coarsely. Puree beets and caraway in food processor.

• Clean green onions and chop finely. Cut chives into rings. Break walnuts into small pieces.

• For rigatoni, bring plenty of water to boil. Add salt and rigatoni and boil until al dente. Reserve 3 to 4 tablespoons cooking water.

• Heat beet puree with green onion rings, walnuts, crème fraîche, reserved rigatoni cooking water, salt, pepper, and lemon juice.

• Drain rigatoni and mix with vegetable puree. Crumble feta cheese and mix with chives. Serve rigatoni sprinkled with feta mixture.

Makes 4 servings.

PER SERVING:	539 CALORIES	
NUTRITIONAL INFORMATION		
Fat (20% calories from fat) 12		g
Protein 22		g
Carbohydrate 87		g
Cholesterol 14		mg
Sodium 7		mg

Tagliatelle with Spinach Pesto

Easy to prepare • Elegant

• For pesto, trim spinach, wash thoroughly, shake dry, and remove coarse stems. Coarsely chop garlic. Drain capers. Dice tomatoes. Dice cheese.

• Combine all ingredients except tagliatelle in food processor or mortar and puree to paste. Season pesto with salt and pepper.

• For tagliatelle, bring plenty of water to boil. Add salt and tagliatelle and boil until al dente. Reserve 3 to 4 tablespoons cooking water.

• Warm a bowl. Add pesto and reserved tagliatelle cooking water and stir until creamy. Drain tagliatelle and toss with pesto. Serve at once.

Makes 4 servings.

PER SERVING:	715 CALORIES	
NUTRITIONAL INFORMATION		
Fat (40% calories from fat) 32		g
Protein 25		g
Carbohydrate 83		g
Cholesterol 8		mg
Sodium 291		mg

Rigatoni with Red Vegetable Cream

2 medium-size red beets (about 1 lb/400 g)
1 teaspoon caraway seeds
2 green onions
1 bunch chives
1 oz (20 g) walnuts
Salt
1 lb (400 g) rigatoni (or tagliatelle)
2 tablespoons crème fraîche or sour cream
Black pepper
2 teaspoons lemon juice
4 oz (100 g) feta cheese

Preparation time: 60 to 70 minutes (40 to 50 minutes cooking time)

Tagliatelle with Spinach Pesto

4 oz (100 g) tender spinach
1 garlic clove
1 teaspoon small capers
2 dried tomatoes, packed in oil
2½ oz (60 g) pecorino or Parmesan
3 oz (80 g) blanched almonds
½ cup (100 ml) olive oil
Salt and pepper
1 lb (400 g) tagliatelle

Preparation time: about 20 minutes

Spaghetti with Raw Vegetables
½ fennel bulb
2 tomatoes
2 young carrots
½ bunch radishes
1 bunch green onions
1 bunch fresh basil
1 garlic clove
¼ cup (60 ml) olive oil
½ dried chili pepper
(optional)
Salt and black pepper
1 lb (400 g) spaghetti

Preparation time: about
30 minutes

Farfalle with Onion Ragout
1 lb (400 g) small red onions
1 orange
1 bunch chives
1 green bell pepper
Salt
1 lb (400 g) farfalle
1 tablespoon butter
½ cup (125 ml) vegetable
broth
2 teaspoons lemon juice
¼ teaspoon crushed saffron
Black pepper
Freshly grated nutmeg
2 oz (50 g) Parmesan in one
piece

Preparation time: about
25 minutes

Spaghetti with Raw Vegetables

Easy to prepare • Light

• Cut fennel lengthwise twice and then across into thin slices. Dip tomatoes in boiling water for a few seconds; peel, halve and dice. Finely grate carrots. Slice radishes and cut slices into thin strips. Cut green onions into thin rings. Cut basil leaves into thin strips. Put garlic through press.

• Mix vegetables with oil and 6 tablespoons water. If desired, stir in crumbled chili pepper. Season with salt and pepper. Cover and set aside.

• For spaghetti, bring plenty of water to boil. Add salt and spaghetti and boil until al dente. Drain and pour into warmed bowl. Toss with vegetable sauce.

Makes 4 servings.

Farfalle with Onion Ragout

Elegant • Pictured

• Cut onions into eighths. Rinse orange with hot water. Cut a strip of the peel and chop finely. Squeeze juice from half of orange. Cut chives into rings. Seed pepper and cut into strips.

• For farfalle, bring plenty of water to boil. Add salt and farfalle and boil until al dente.

• Melt butter in pot. Sauté onion wedges until translucent. Stir in pepper strips. Deglaze pan with orange juice and broth. Stir in lemon juice and saffron. Season with salt, pepper, and nutmeg. Simmer, covered, over medium heat 10 minutes.

• Drain farfalle. Season onion ragout with orange peel and chives. Mix with farfalle. Divide among warmed plates. Shave Parmesan over top.

Makes 4 servings.

PER SERVING:	444 CALORIES
NUTRITIONAL INFORMATION	
Fat (12% calories from fat) 7	g
Protein 22	g
Carbohydrate 82	g
Cholesterol 0	mg
Sodium 4	mg

PER SERVING:	517 CALORIES
NUTRITIONAL INFORMATION	
Fat (14% calories from fat) 8	g
Protein 20	g
Carbohydrate 90	g
Cholesterol 14	mg
Sodium 229	mg

Macaroni with Dandelion Greens

1 lb (400 g) dandelion greens
Salt
9 oz (250 g) tomatoes
3 oz (80 g) black olives
2 garlic cloves
1 lb (400 g) macaroni
1 tablespoon olive oil
1 tablespoon pine nuts
1 tablespoon capers
1 dried chili pepper
Freshly grated pecorino

Preparation time: about
30 minutes

Tagliatelle with Lemon Sauce

1 bunch green onions
1 carrot
1 garlic clove
1 bunch mixed fresh herbs
1 package garden cress or
sprouts
Salt
1 lb (400 g) tagliatelle
1 tablespoon olive oil
3 tablespoons lemon juice
2 tablespoons crème fraîche
or sour cream
Cayenne pepper

Preparation time: about
25 minutes

Macaroni with Dandelion Greens

Elegant • Pictured

• Trim dandelion greens and cut into 1-in (2.5 cm) pieces. Blanch in boiling water 3 minutes. Rinse with cold water and drain. Core tomatoes. Dip in boiling water, peel, and cut into small cubes. Cut olives into thin strips. Mince garlic.

• For macaroni, bring plenty of water to boil. Add salt and macaroni and boil until al dente.

• Heat olive oil in pan and sauté pine nuts and garlic until golden. Stir in tomatoes, olives, capers, and crumbled chili pepper. Cook uncovered over medium heat 5 minutes. Stir in dandelion greens, salt, and pepper. Cover and cook an additional 2 minutes.

• Drain macaroni, mix with vegetable ragout, and serve sprinkled with pecorino.

Makes 4 servings.

PER SERVING:	500 CALORIES	
NUTRITIONAL INFORMATION		
Fat (15% calories from fat) 8		g
Protein 17		g
Carbohydrate 88		g
Cholesterol 1		mg
Sodium 207		mg

Tagliatelle with Lemon Sauce

Economical • Light

• Clean green onions and cut into 2-in (5 cm) pieces, then into thin strips. Trim and peel carrot and cut into julienne strips. Mince garlic and herbs. Trim cress and mix with herbs. Set aside a small amount for garnish.

• For tagliatelle, bring plenty of water to boil. Add salt and tagliatelle and boil until al dente. Reserve 3 to 4 tablespoons cooking water.

• Heat olive oil in pan and sauté onions, carrot, and garlic until softened. Add lemon juice and reserved tagliatelle cooking water. Cover and cook over medium heat about 3 minutes. Stir in herbs, crème fraîche, salt, and pepper.

• Drain tagliatelle and immediately mix with sauce. Serve sprinkled with reserved herbs.

Makes 4 servings.

PER SERVING:	419 CALORIES	
NUTRITIONAL INFORMATION		
Fat (12% calories from fat) 6		g
Protein 14		g
Carbohydrate 80		g
Cholesterol 4		mg
Sodium 0		mg

Spaghetti with Bread Crumbs

1 bunch fresh basil
2 medium tomatoes
Salt
1 lb (400 g) spaghetti
¼ cup (60 ml) olive oil
4 heaping tablespoons dry
bread crumbs (made from
whole-grain bread)
Freshly ground white pepper

Preparation time: about
20 minutes

Rigatoni with Horseradish Sauce

10 oz (300 g) parsley roots
or young parsnips
1 large bunch Italian parsley
Salt
1 pound (400 g) rigatoni
1 tablespoon butter
1 scant cup (200 ml)
vegetable broth
1 piece fresh horseradish,
1 inch (2.5 cm) long
10 tablespoons crème fraîche
or sour cream
Black pepper

Preparation time: about
35 minutes

Spaghetti with Bread Crumbs

Elegant • Pictured

• Cut basil leaves into thin strips. Core tomatoes and cut into small cubes.

• For spaghetti, bring plenty of water to boil. Add salt and spaghetti and boil until al dente. Reserve 6 tablespoons cooking water.

• Heat oil in pan and sauté bread crumbs over medium heat until golden. Add basil and tomatoes and stir only until hot. Add reserved spaghetti cooking water and stir until smooth and thick. Season with salt and pepper.

• Drain spaghetti and stir into crumb mixture. Serve at once.

Makes 4 servings.

Rigatoni with Horseradish Sauce

Economical • Elegant

• Peel parsley roots and cut into julienne. Tear off parsley leaves and set aside. Finely chop only the tender stems.

• For rigatoni, bring plenty of water to boil. Add salt and rigatoni and boil until al dente.

• Melt butter in pot and sauté parsley roots and chopped parsley stems until golden. Pour in broth, cover, and cook over medium heat about 5 minutes.

• Peel horseradish and grate or puree in food processor. Chop reserved parsley leaves. Add horseradish, parsley, and crème fraîche to parsley roots and heat through. Season with salt and pepper.

• Drain rigatoni and stir into sauce.

Makes 4 servings.

40

PER SERVING:	472 CALORIES	
NUTRITIONAL INFORMATION		
Fat (19% calories from fat) 10		g
Protein 14		g
Carbohydrate 80		g
Cholesterol 0		mg
Sodium 11		mg

PER SERVING:	604 CALORIES	
NUTRITIONAL INFORMATION		
Fat (31% calories from fat) 20		g
Protein 17		g
Carbohydrate 86		g
Cholesterol 57		mg
Sodium 356		mg

Orzo with Eggplant Ragout

Pictured • Easy

- Trim eggplant and cut into cubes. Halve onion and cut into thin slices. Core tomato; dip into boiling water for a few seconds and peel. Cut into small cubes. Clean peppers and cut into thin strips.

- Heat oil in nonstick skillet and sauté eggplant over medium heat until golden. Add onion, peppers, and tomato and cook, covered, over low heat 6 to 8 minutes.

- For orzo, bring plenty of water to boil. Add salt and orzo and boil until al dente.

- Peel garlic and put through press. Mix yogurt with garlic, parsley, salt, and pepper.

- Drain orzo and stir into eggplant mixture. Season with salt and pepper. Serve topped with yogurt mixture.

Makes 4 servings.

PER SERVING:	500 CALORIES	
NUTRITIONAL INFORMATION		
Fat (25% calories from fat) 14	g
Protein 17	g
Carbohydrate 79	g
Cholesterol 97	mg
Sodium 6	mg

Spaghetti with Chicory Ragout

Economical • Quick

- Finely chop shallots. Halve chicory lengthwise. Remove core and cut chicory into strips.

- For spaghetti, bring plenty of water to boil. Add salt and spaghetti and boil until al dente.

- Heat oil in pot and sauté shallots until translucent. Add chicory and walnuts and sauté briefly. Stir in cream. Season with salt, pepper, nutmeg, and lemon juice. Cover and cook over low heat about 5 minutes.

- Finely chop parsley. Drain spaghetti and mix with parsley and chicory ragout. Serve on warmed plates.

Makes 4 servings.

PER SERVING:	542 CALORIES	
NUTRITIONAL INFORMATION		
Fat (29% calories from fat) 18	g
Protein 15	g
Carbohydrate 81	g
Cholesterol 41	mg
Sodium 1	mg

Orzo with Eggplant Ragout

1 generous lb (500 g) young eggplant
1 white onion
1 beefsteak tomato
2 to 4 green bell peppers
5 tablespoons olive oil
Salt
1 lb (400 g) orzo
3 garlic cloves
½ cup (100 ml) plain yogurt
2 tablespoons chopped parsley
Black pepper

Preparation time: about 35 minutes

Spaghetti with Chicory Ragout

2 shallots
10 oz (300 g) chicory
Salt
1 lb (400 g) spaghetti (or rigatoni)
1 tablespoon oil
1 tablespoon coarsely chopped walnuts
¾ cup (150 ml) heavy cream
Black pepper
Freshly grated nutmeg
1 teaspoon lemon juice
½ bunch parsley

Preparation time: about 25 minutes

Stir-Fried Noodles with Vegetables

Easy • Asian-inspired

• Soak mushrooms in lukewarm water 30 minutes. Drain and cut off hard stems. Depending on size, quarter or halve caps.

• For noodles, bring plenty of water to boil. Add salt and noodles and boil until tender but still firm. Rinse with cold water and drain.

• Trim tough ends from asparagus and cut into 1½-in (3–4 cm) pieces. Blanch asparagus and snow peas in salted boiling water 3 minutes. Rinse with cold water and drain.

• Halve pepper, clean, and cut into strips. Trim squash, halve lengthwise, and slice. Finely chop garlic. Tear off basil leaves.

• Heat 2 tablespoons oil in large skillet and sauté vegetables, garlic, and sprouts over medium heat about 5 minutes.

• Heat remaining oil in another large skillet or wok and stir-fry noodles over medium to high heat until brown and crisp.

• Season vegetables with rice wine, basil, soy sauce, salt, and pepper. Finely chop peanuts.

• Mix noodles with vegetables and season again with salt and pepper. Serve sprinkled with peanuts.

Makes 4 servings.

Tip:

To simplify this dish, use a package of frozen Chinese vegetables and stir-fry over high heat until crisp-tender.

10 dried shiitake mushrooms
Salt
1 lb (400 g) Chinese egg noodles
4 oz (100 g) asparagus
4 oz (100 g) snow peas
1 red bell pepper
1 summer squash
2 garlic cloves
1 bunch fresh basil
6 tablespoons peanut oil
4 oz (100 g) mung bean sprouts
2 tablespoons rice wine (or water)
2 tablespoons soy sauce
Pepper
2 tablespoons peanuts

Preparation time: about 1 hour and 10 minutes (30 minutes boiling time)

PER SERVING:	625 CALORIES	
NUTRITIONAL INFORMATION		
Fat (38% calories from fat) 27		g
Protein 18		g
Carbohydrate 80		g
Cholesterol 94		mg
Sodium 586		mg

Rice Noodles with Coconut Spinach

Elegant • Asian-inspired

• Peel ginger and garlic and chop finely. Finely crumble chili pepper. Halve onion and cut into strips. Clean leek, wash well, and chop finely.

• Drain spinach and squeeze as dry as possible. Heat oil in pan and sauté ginger, garlic, onion, leek, and crumbled chili over medium heat 3 to 4 minutes. Add coconut milk, soy sauce, spinach, and lemon juice and simmer 5 minutes.

• For noodles, bring plenty of water to boil. Add salt and noodles and boil 3 to 4 minutes or until tender but still firm. Rinse with cold water and drain. Stir noodles into spinach mixture and heat through.

Makes 4 servings.

PER SERVING:	465 CALORIES
NUTRITIONAL INFORMATION	

Fat (14% calories from fat) . . . . 10 g
Protein . . . . 39 g
Carbohydrate . . . . 109 g
Cholesterol . . . . 0 mg
Sodium . . . . 1050 mg

Rice Noodles with Tofu Tartare

Pictured • Light

• Clean green onions and chop finely with tender green parts. Clean red pepper and dice finely. Trim green beans and cut diagonally into thin slices. Drain tofu and chop finely. Toast sesame seeds in dry pan over medium heat until aromatic.

• Heat peanut oil in pan and sauté vegetables and tofu over medium heat about 5 minutes. Stir in vegetable broth and soy sauce.

• For noodles, bring plenty of water to boil. Add salt and rice noodles and cook 3 minutes or until tender but still firm.

• Drain noodles and stir into vegetables. Season with sambal oelek, salt, and lemon juice. Serve sprinkled with sesame seeds and cilantro leaves.

Makes 4 servings.

PER SERVING:	508 CALORIES
NUTRITIONAL INFORMATION	

Fat (30% calories from fat) . . . . 18 g
Protein . . . . 21 g
Carbohydrate . . . . 74 g
Cholesterol . . . . 0 mg
Sodium . . . . 1893 mg

Rice Noodles with Coconut Spinach

1 walnut-size piece fresh ginger root
2 garlic cloves
1 dried chili pepper
1 onion
1 leek (about 3 oz/75 g)
1 pkg (10 oz/283 g) frozen chopped spinach, thawed
2 tablespoons peanut oil
1 scant cup (200 ml) canned coconut milk or coconut cream
1 tablespoon soy sauce
2 teaspoons lemon juice
Salt
1 lb (400 g) wide rice noodles

Preparation time: about 25 minutes

Rice Noodles with Tofu Tartare

1 bunch green onions
1 red bell pepper
4 oz (100 g) broad green beans
9 oz (250 g) firm tofu
2 tablespoons sesame seeds
3 tablespoons peanut oil
½ cup (125 ml) vegetable broth
3 tablespoons light soy sauce
Salt
12 oz (350 g) thin rice noodles
1 teaspoon sambal oelek
2 tablespoons lemon juice
Fresh cilantro (coriander) leaves for garnish

Preparation time: about 45 minutes

47

very
special

Homemade Noodles

Homemade noodles have the undeserved reputation of being very complicated, but they're simple to make with the help of a pasta machine. With a little extra effort, make a double batch and dry a portion of the finished noodles for future use.

Noodle Dough (basic recipe for 4 servings)

Dough can be prepared using only a few staple ingredients. Place 2⅔ cups (400 g) all-purpose or bread flour (or half all-purpose and half semolina flour) in a bowl with 4 eggs, 1 scant teaspoon salt, and 1 tablespoon oil. Stir to incorporate flour, then knead on a floured surface about 5 minutes or until smooth, shiny, and not sticky. If the dough is too dry, add water drop by drop until you have a dough that is smooth and elastic; alternatively, add an extra egg yolk. If dough is too sticky, gradually stir in more flour.

For easier mixing and kneading, use a mixer with a dough hook, a food processor, or a pasta machine. (If using a pasta machine, set rollers on widest setting and run dough through machine. Fold dough in thirds and repeat several times until dough is smooth and elastic. Dust dough lightly with flour each time it is rolled.)

Wrap dough in plastic or a damp kitchen towel and let rest at room temperature 30 minutes, then knead again and cut into pieces as directed in recipe. Any dough that is waiting to be shaped should be wrapped to prevent drying.

Shaping Noodles

With a pasta machine, make the roller settings progressively narrower until dough is desired thinness, dusting dough with flour each time it is rolled. Then use the machine to cut the dough into noodles. By hand, use a lightly floured rolling pin to roll dough on a lightly floured surface into a paper-thin sheet. Cut into noodles with a sharp knife, pizza cutter, or pastry wheel.

Spread noodles on a lightly floured kitchen towel and let dry for a few hours, turning occasionally to permit even drying. Freshly made noodles can be cooked immediately, allowing a shorter cooking time.

Cook noodles in plenty of salted boiling water 1 to 3 minutes or until al dente. Timing should start after the water returns to a boil when the pasta is added.

With Whole-Grain Flour

Preparation of noodle dough using whole-grain flour is no extra trouble. The dough will require a little more liquid; add an extra egg yolk or mix in a little extra water.

You can substitute other flours, such as buckwheat, millet, oat, or rye using one-third to one-half the total amount of flour in the recipe.

Without Egg

Mix 1 cup (150 g) all-purpose flour and 1 cup (150 g) semolina (durum hard wheat flour) with 1 teaspoon salt and ½ cup (125 ml) lukewarm water until smooth. Knead thoroughly on a floured surface until elastic. Cover and let dough rest about 1 hour before shaping as desired.

Colorful Additions

Delicious noodle dough can be colored or flavored with many additions.

• Yellow: Add ½ teaspoon powdered saffron with the eggs

• Orange: Knead in 2 tablespoons tomato paste. Use 1 less egg.

• Red: Cook 1 small red beet until tender. Peel and puree. Stir beet puree and only 2 eggs into flour. If necessary, stir in more flour.

• Green: Blanch 7 oz (200 g) spinach in boiling salted water. Rinse with cold water. Drain. Squeeze spinach very firmly with hands or towel to remove all excess liquid. Puree in a food mill or processor. Stir puree and only 2 eggs into flour. Depending on moisture in spinach, knead in a little extra flour, if necessary.

• Aromatic: Soak ½ oz (10–20 g) dried mushrooms in warm water 30 minutes. Drain, mince, and knead into dough.

• Spicy: Knead in 1 to 2 dried chilies, ground to powder in a mortar, or 2 teaspoons crushed red pepper flakes.

Storage

If you wish to store homemade noodles, they must be well dried. Hang long noodles like linguine or tagliatelle over a taut cord or clean broom handle to dry. Store in large airtight jars. Cook about 8 minutes as for purchased noodles.

Noodles make a very personal gift. Pack them in a glass jar or attractive bag. Prepare a pesto (page 27 or 35) and package them together, tied with ribbons and including directions for cooking.

Orecchiette with Asparagus Arugula Ragout

For company • Easy to prepare

• For orecchiette, mix flours and salt in bowl. Mix in oil and add water gradually until smooth (see page 50). Knead dough on floured surface until smooth and elastic. Shape into ball and wrap in kitchen towel. Let stand at room temperature about 30 minutes.

• Knead dough again and cut into 4 pieces. Shape each piece on lightly floured surface into long roll the thickness of a finger. Cut rolls into slices ¼ inch (3 mm) thick. With floured thumb, press dough down in center of slice until shaped like a tiny hat or small ear. Spread noodles on kitchen towel and dry overnight.

• For ragout, trim tough ends from asparagus. Cut off tips and reserve. Thinly peel asparagus and cut into 1-in (2.5 cm) pieces.

• Bring plenty of water to boil with salt and sugar. Add asparagus pieces and cook 3 minutes. Add tips and cook another 5 minutes. Remove with slotted spoon.

• Core tomato and blanch in asparagus cooking water for a few seconds. Remove tomato and rinse with cold water. Peel and cut into small cubes.

• Trim arugula and chop coarsely. Mince garlic.

• Heat oil in pot and sauté garlic until golden. Add arugula and tomato and cook uncovered over medium heat 10 minutes. Season with salt and cayenne.

• For orecchiette, bring plenty of water to boil. Add salt and orecchiette and boil 8 to 10 minutes (depending on drying time) until al dente.

• Stir asparagus into arugula mixture and reheat. Drain orecchiette and stir into asparagus ragout. Serve immediately on warmed plates.

Makes 4 servings.

For Orecchiette:
1 cup (150 g) durum wheat flour (semolina or bread flour)
1 cup (150 g) all-purpose flour
1 teaspoon salt
2 tablespoons olive oil
About ½ cup (125 ml) lukewarm water
Flour for work surface

For Ragout:
1 lb (500 g) asparagus
Salt
Sugar
1 beefsteak tomato
2 bunches arugula
2 garlic cloves
1 tablespoon olive oil
Cayenne pepper

Preparation time: about 1¼ hours (plus drying time)

PER SERVING:	347 CALORIES
NUTRITIONAL INFORMATION	
Fat (18% calories from fat) 7	g
Protein 12	g
Carbohydrate 59	g
Cholesterol 0	mg
Sodium 24	mg

For Noodles:
2 cups (300 g) semolina or
all-purpose flour
Salt
1 tablespoon olive oil
3 eggs
1 additional egg yolk, if
needed
Few sprigs fresh chervil
Flour for work surface

For Sauce:
1 lb (500 g) tomatoes
1 shallot
2 garlic cloves
1 tablespoon butter
⅔ cup (150 ml) crème
fraîche, or ½ cup (125 ml)
heavy cream and ¼ cup
(60 ml) sour cream
Salt and black pepper
¼ teaspoon honey
2 oz (50 g) pecorino in one
piece

Preparation time: about
1 hour (plus 1 hour resting
time)

Chervil Noodles with Tomato Cream
Elegant • For Company

• Mix flour, ½ teaspoon salt, oil, and eggs until smooth. Knead on floured surface to form smooth dough (see page 50). Add a little extra flour if too moist or an extra egg yolk if too dry. Wrap dough in plastic and let rest at room temperature 30 minutes.

• Trim chervil; pull leaves from stems. Make sure leaves are well dried.

• Knead dough again and cut into 2 pieces. Roll out each piece on lightly floured surface as thin as possible into 2 equal-size sheets. Sprinkle one sheet with chervil leaves and cover with second sheet. Roll dough out again as thin as possible. Cut sheet of dough into noodles 1 in (2.5 cm) wide. Place noodles side by side on lightly floured kitchen towel at least 30 minutes.

• For sauce, core tomatoes, dip into boiling water, peel, and cut into quarters. Remove seeds and cut tomatoes into small cubes. Mince shallot and garlic.

• Melt butter in pot and sauté shallot and garlic until golden. Add tomatoes and sauté briefly.

• Stir in crème fraîche and season with salt, pepper, and honey. Cook uncovered over medium heat about 10 minutes.

• For noodles, bring plenty of water to boil. Add salt and noodles and cook 1 to 3 minutes or until al dente.

• Drain noodles and place on warmed plates. Spoon sauce over noodles. Sprinkle with pecorino shavings and serve at once.

Makes 4 servings.

Tip:
Noodles also look attractive with larger herb leaves, such as basil, sage, or marjoram.

PER SERVING:	577 CALORIES
NUTRITIONAL INFORMATION	
Fat (45% calories from fat) 29	g
Protein 19	g
Carbohydrate 61	g
Cholesterol 298	mg
Sodium 15	mg

Buckwheat Noodles with Calvados Mushrooms

Fast to prepare • Light

• For noodles, mix flours with 1 teaspoon salt and lukewarm water until smooth (see page 50). Knead until smooth and elastic. Shape dough into ball, wrap in plastic and let rest at room temperature 30 minutes.

• Knead dough again and cut into 4 pieces. Roll out each piece on floured work surface as thin as possible, or roll out in pasta machine. Cut dough into noodles ½ inch (1 cm) wide. Spread out on floured kitchen towel.

• For ragout, trim mushrooms and brush clean with paper towel. Cut into slices or strips. Mince garlic. Strip thyme leaves from stems.

• For noodles, bring plenty of water to boil. Add salt and noodles and boil 2 to 3 minutes or until al dente.

• Heat oil in pan and sauté mushrooms, garlic, and thyme over medium heat until all liquid has evaporated.

• Place Calvados in ladle and warm over very low heat. Using long matchstick, set aflame and pour over mushrooms. When flames die, stir in cream and season with salt, pepper, and cloves. Stir in lemon peel.

• Drain noodles and place on warmed plates. Divide mushrooms among plates. Sprinkle with thyme and strips of lemon peel. Serve at once.

Makes 4 servings.

For Noodles:
1⅔ cups (250 g) semolina or spelt flour (sold in health food stores)
1 cup (150 g) buckwheat flour
Salt
1 scant cup (200 ml) lukewarm water
Flour for work surface

For Ragout:
1½ lbs (600 g) mixed wild mushrooms (shiitake, crimini, cepes, chanterelles, oyster, porcini, small portobellos)
2 garlic cloves
Few sprigs fresh thyme
1 tablespoon olive oil
¼ cup (60 ml) Calvados (apple brandy)
1 scant cup (200 ml) heavy cream
Salt and black pepper
Pinch of ground cloves
¼ teaspoon grated lemon peel
Thyme sprigs and strips of lemon peel for garnish

Preparation time: about 1 hour (plus 30 minutes resting time)

PER SERVING:	592 CALORIES	
NUTRITIONAL INFORMATION		
Fat (33% calories from fat) 21	g
Protein 18	g
Carbohydrate 76	g
Cholesterol 55	mg
Sodium 9	mg

For Spaetzle:
1⅔ cups (250 g) whole-wheat or spelt flour (sold in health food stores)
¾–1 cup (125 g) fine rye flour (sold in health food stores)
Salt
3 eggs
1 cup (250 ml) cold water

For Vegetables:
4 young kohlrabi (about 1½ lbs/700 g)
1 bunch arugula
Few leaves lemon balm
1 cup (250 ml) sour cream or heavy cream
Salt and black pepper
1 tablespoon clarified butter
1 tablespoon butter

Preparation time: about 50 minutes

Wheat and Rye Spaetzle with Kohlrabi
Economical • Elegant

Spaetzle are long, string-like dumplings.

• For spaetzle, mix flours with 1 teaspoon salt in bowl or mixer with dough hook. Add eggs and beat to form thick dough. Gradually beat in water until dough is consistency of muffin batter. Let stand at room temperature 30 minutes.

• For vegetables, peel kohlrabi and cut into ½-in (1 cm) slices. Cut slices into sticks. Reserve tender kohlrabi greens.

• Cut arugula and lemon balm into thin strips. Stir into sour cream along with 2 tablespoons cold water. Season with salt and pepper.

• For spaetzle, bring plenty of salted water to boil. Pour spaetzle dough into spaetzle maker (similar in shape to a food mill) and let dough fall into simmering water (see back folded cover). Alternatively, place dough on cutting board. Place knife at edge of dough and scrape thin strips of dough off board and into water. Cook spaetzle until they rise to surface. Remove with slotted spoon, drain, and keep warm in preheated 200°F (50°C) oven.

• Heat clarified butter in pan and sauté kohlrabi over medium heat, stirring occasionally, about 10 minutes or until crisp-tender and lightly browned.

• Finely chop reserved kohlrabi greens. Stir into kohlrabi and season with salt and pepper.

• Heat butter in large pan. Fold in spaetzle and heat through. Spoon spaetzle onto warmed plates. Top with kohlrabi and sour cream and herb sauce.

Makes 4 servings.

PER SERVING:	531 CALORIES	
NUTRITIONAL INFORMATION		
Fat (30% calories from fat) 18	g	
Protein 23	g	
Carbohydrate 70	g	
Cholesterol 269	mg	
Sodium 11	mg	

For Noodles:

½ teaspoon crushed saffron
2 cups (300 g) all-purpose flour
Salt
1 tablespoon olive oil
3 eggs
1 additional egg yolk, if needed
Flour for work surface

For Vegetables:

1½ lbs (700 g) beet greens
1 bunch green onions
1 bunch parsley
1 bunch peppermint
Salt
3 tablespoons olive oil
Black pepper
Freshly grated nutmeg
2 teaspoons lemon juice
2 oz (50 g) pecorino in one piece

Preparation time: about 1 hour (plus 1 hour resting time)

Saffron Noodle Diamonds with Beet Greens

Easy to prepare • Elegant

• For noodles, mix saffron with 1 tablespoon water. In bowl, mix flour, ½ teaspoon salt, olive oil, eggs, and saffron mixture and knead to form smooth dough (see page 50). If too dry, mix in an extra egg yolk. If too moist, stir in extra flour. Shape dough into ball, wrap in plastic, and let rest at room temperature 30 minutes.

• Knead dough again and cut into 2 pieces. Roll out each piece on floured surface as thin as possible. Cut into diamonds. Spread diamonds on floured kitchen towel and let dry 30 minutes.

• Trim beet greens and coarsely chop leaves. Cut stems into thin strips. Clean green onions and cut into thin rings. Tear off herb leaves. Set aside a small amount of each herb; finely chop remaining herbs.

• Bring plenty of salted water to boil. Add beet stems and cook 3 minutes. Add beet leaves, onions, and chopped herbs and cook another 3 minutes.

• Drain in sieve, rinse with cold water, and drain. Finely chop reserved herbs.

• Bring plenty of water to boil. Add salt and noodles and cook 1 to 3 minutes or until al dente.

• Heat oil in pan. Add drained vegetables and chopped raw herbs. Season with salt, pepper, nutmeg, and lemon juice and sauté until hot.

• Drain noodles well and stir into greens. Serve on warmed plates. Shave pecorino over top. Serve at once.

Makes 4 servings.

PER SERVING:	466 CALORIES	
NUTRITIONAL INFORMATION		
Fat (35% calories from fat) 18		g
Protein 21		g
Carbohydrate 57		g
Cholesterol 241		mg
Sodium 0		mg

Fettuccine with Green Onions

For company • Easy to prepare

• For fettucine, mix flour, ½ teaspoon salt, 1 tablespoon oil, and eggs and knead to form smooth dough (see page 50). If too dry, add another egg yolk. If too moist, add more flour. Shape dough into ball, wrap in plastic, and let rest at room temperature about 30 minutes.

• Knead dough again and cut into 2 pieces. Roll out each piece on floured surface as thin as possible. Cut into ½-in (1 cm) strips. Spread out on floured kitchen towel and dry about 30 minutes.

• Clean green onions and cut lengthwise into thin strips.

• For fettuccine, bring plenty of water to boil. Add salt and fettuccine and boil 1 to 3 minutes or until al dente. Reserve 2 tablespoons cooking water.

• Heat oil in pan and sauté green onions until translucent. Stir in crème fraîche and reserved fettuccine cooking water. Season with salt and pepper. Cover and keep warm over very low heat.

• Drain fettuccine well. Add to green onion mixture. Stir in 1 tablespoon truffle oil. Serve on warmed plates and sprinkle each serving with remaining truffle oil. Serve at once.

Makes 4 servings.

Variation:
Thick Homemade Spaghetti

Mix 2 cups (300 g) all-purpose flour with 1 teaspoon salt and ¾ to 1 cup (200–275 ml) water to form firm and pliable dough (see page 50). Shape into ball, wrap in plastic, and let rest at room temperature about 30 minutes. Knead dough again and cut into olive-size pieces. With hands, roll each piece on floured surface into spaghetti-like strand. Drop into salted boiling water and boil 3 minutes or until al dente. This is especially good with a simple tomato sauce or mushroom ragout.

For Fettuccine:
3 cups (300 g) all-purpose flour
Salt
1 tablespoon olive oil
3 eggs
1 egg yolk (optional)
Flour for work surface

For Vegetables:
2 bunches green onions
1½ teaspoons olive oil
2 tablespoons crème fraîche (or sour cream)
Salt
Black pepper
Few chervil leaves
About 2 tablespoons truffle oil

Preparation time: about 50 minutes (plus 1 hour resting time)

PER SERVING:	388 CALORIES
NUTRITIONAL INFORMATION	

Fat (29% calories from fat) 13   g
Protein 15   g
Carbohydrate 56   g
Cholesterol 240   mg
Sodium 2   mg

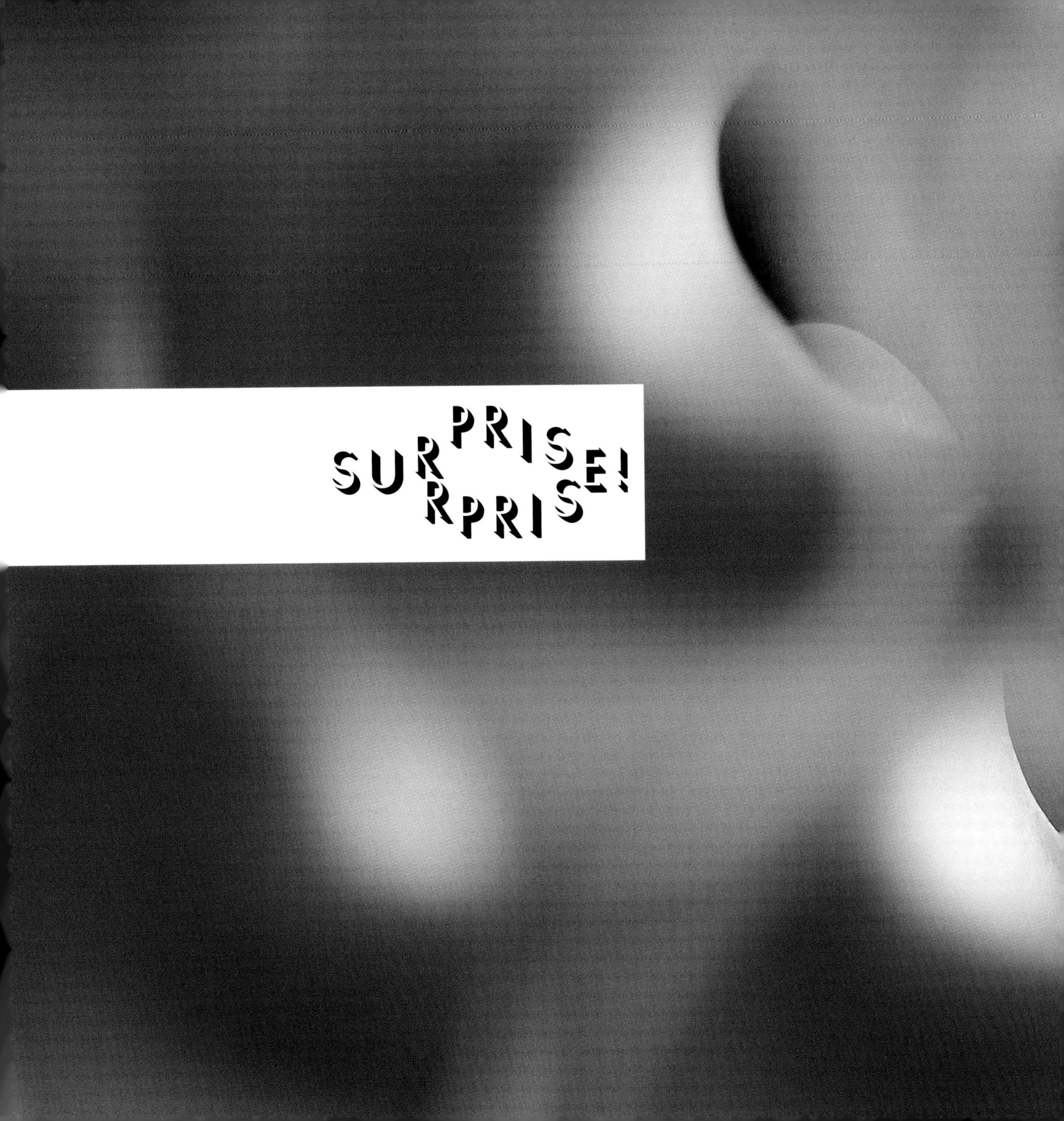
PRISE
SURR E!
RPRIS

Delicate Filled Noodles

A combination of delicate dough and moist filling, homemade stuffed pasta always makes an impression. Best of all, it lends itself to preparation a day ahead.

Filled noodles made perfectly

First prepare dough as directed on page 50, kneading it well. Let dough rest, then roll it into a paper-thin sheet with a rolling pin or pasta machine.

The dough should be divided into small portions; if rolled out all at once, it will dry out by the time you finish filling it. The filled noodles will be difficult to shape and seal, and will open during cooking.

The thinner the dough is rolled, the easier you will find it to enclose the delicate filling. When using a rolling pin, allow plenty of time for rolling the dough.

Use a pastry wheel, pizza cutter, or knife to cut dough into squares or triangles.

Dough rounds can be cut with a cookie cutter or a thin-walled glass; all utensils used for cutting should be dipped in flour. (Helpful hints are listed in the back folded cover.) Place small amount of filling in the middle of each piece of dough, allowing a ½-in (1 cm) border all around the filling to allow for folding and sealing.

Before sealing, brush edges of dough with water or lightly beaten egg white to prevent opening during cooking. After shaping, press edges of dough together firmly with the floured tines of a fork.

Different Shapes

• Roll out a large rectangle of dough. Spoon filling in teaspoon-size mounds on half of the dough and brush between mounds with water. Fold over the other half of the dough, pressing between the mounds to enclose filling. (If you prefer, work with two equal-size sheets of dough, and sandwich them.) Cut into squares using a sharp knife or pastry wheel. Press edges firmly to seal.

• For half moons, cut the sheet of dough into rounds. Place a mound of filling in the center of each round, brush edges with water, and fold over to enclose the filling. Press edges together.

• "Little hats," or cappelletti, can be made by pressing the ends of half-moon shapes together above the filling.

• For tortellini, put filling on squares of dough. Brush edges with water and fold over, forming a triangle. Firmly press edges together. Wrap the ends of the longest side of the triangle around a finger, pressing firmly to seal at points. Fold over the point of the triangle to seal in the filling. Carefully remove finger.

For Storage

Preparing filled noodles requires extra effort and, most of all, time. It makes sense to prepare a big batch for storage.

Any filled noodles that aren't eaten immediately can be placed side by side on a cookie sheet and frozen. When hard, transfer to a freezer container with tightly sealed lid. Store in freezer no longer than three months.

To cook, bring plenty of salted water to boil in a large pot. Add frozen filled noodles and cook 3 to 5 minutes after water returns to boil.

To prepare filled noodles the night before, cut, fill, and shape as desired. Place side by side on a cookie sheet lined with a lightly floured kitchen towel. Cover with another towel to keep them from drying completely. Store in a cool place overnight.

Two cooking methods

Most filled noodles are simply cooked in salted boiling water. They can also be steamed in a covered basket or perforated pot set over boiling water. Asian noodles are cooked in this manner. Steaming is also the best method for reheating leftover filled noodles.

Dough for Asian filled noodles

Asian filled noodles are made of dough without eggs. Most consist of flour, salt, and lukewarm water mixed and kneaded into a smooth dough. The dough has a delicate flavor that combines well with richly flavored fillings. Dough made with just water is more fragile than dough made with eggs, so it is best cooked by steaming; the noodles would split open easily in boiling water.

Mascarpone Tortellini with Pepper Ragout

Takes time • Easy to prepare

• For dough, mix flour, eggs, oil, and salt and knead to form smooth, elastic dough (see page 50). Shape into ball, cover with towel or wrap in plastic, and let rest at room temperature about 30 minutes.

• For filling, cut mozzarella into tiny cubes. Mix mascarpone with Parmesan and egg yolk. Stir in mozzarella cubes. Season with salt, pepper, nutmeg, and lemon juice.

• Knead dough again. Roll out on lightly floured surface until paper thin. Cut into 2-in (5 cm) rounds using floured cookie cutter. Place ½ teaspoon filling on center of each round. Brush edges of dough rounds with water.

• Fold dough over filling and press edges together. Pull ends of fold lightly, wrap around finger and press points firmly together. Place on floured kitchen towel.

• For ragout, halve, trim, and cube peppers. Core tomatoes. Dip in boiling water, peel, quarter, and finely dice. Mince onion.

• For tortellini, bring plenty of salted water to boil. Boil tortellini 3 to 5 minutes or until al dente.

• For ragout, heat oil in deep pan and sauté until translucent. Add peppers and sauté a few minutes. Stir in tomatoes and season with salt, pepper, and paprika. Cover and cook over low heat 5 to 10 minutes.

• Drain tortellini and place on warmed plates. Top with pepper ragout and serve at once with grated Parmesan cheese.

Makes 4 servings.

For Dough:
2 cups (300 g) all-purpose flour
3 eggs
1 tablespoon olive oil
1 teaspoon salt
Flour for work surface

For Filling:
4 oz (125 g) mozzarella
9 oz (250 g) mascarpone
2 oz (50 g) Parmesan, freshly grated
1 egg yolk
Salt
Black pepper
Freshly grated nutmeg
2 teaspoons lemon juice

For Ragout:
1¾ lbs (800 g) bell peppers, mixed colors
9 oz (250 g) tomatoes
1 white onion
1 tablespoon olive oil
Salt and black pepper
Hot paprika
Freshly grated Parmesan for topping

Preparation time: about 2 hours

PER SERVING:	839 CALORIES
NUTRITIONAL INFORMATION	
Fat (53% calories from fat) 50	g
Protein 31	g
Carbohydrate 67	g
Cholesterol 407	mg
Sodium 7	mg

For Dough:

2⅔ cups (400 g) all-purpose flour
4 eggs
1 tablespoon olive oil
1 teaspoon salt
Flour for work surface

For Filling:

1¾ lbs (750 g) white asparagus
Salt
Pinch of sugar
1 shallot
1 handful fresh chervil
3 tablespoons pine nuts
1 small egg
4 oz (100 g) pecorino, freshly grated
2 to 3 tablespoons dry bread crumbs
Pepper
Freshly grated nutmeg

For Sauce:

1 handful fresh chervil
4 oz (1 stick/100 g) butter
Pepper

Preparation time: about 2 hours

Ravioli with Asparagus Filling

For company • Easy to prepare

• For dough, mix flour with eggs, oil, and salt and knead to form smooth, elastic dough (see page 50). Shape dough into ball, wrap in plastic, and let rest at room temperature about 30 minutes.

• For filling, trim woody ends from asparagus and cut off tips. Peel asparagus and cut into 1-in (2.5 cm) pieces. Bring plenty of water to boil with salt and sugar. Add asparagus pieces and simmer 8 minutes. Add tips and simmer another 5 minutes. Drain well and set tips aside.

• Peel and grate shallot. Cut chervil leaves into thin strips. Finely chop pine nuts.

• Puree asparagus pieces and mix with shallot, chervil, pine nuts, egg, pecorino, and crumbs. Season with salt, pepper, and nutmeg.

• Knead dough again and cut into 4 pieces. Roll each piece on floured surface until paper thin. Cut into 2½-in (6 cm) squares. Spoon 2 teaspoons asparagus filling in center of each square. Brush edges with water and fold over, shaping a rectangle or triangle. Press edges together.

• Bring plenty of salted water to boil. Boil ravioli 3 to 4 minutes. Remove from heat but leave ravioli in the water.

• For sauce, tear off leaves from chervil. Heat butter until lightly browned. Add asparagus tips. Stir in chervil and pepper to taste.

• Remove ravioli from water using slotted spoon. Place on warmed plates. Spoon butter mixture over ravioli. Serve at once.

Makes 4 to 6 servings.

PER SERVING:	558 CALORIES	
NUTRITIONAL INFORMATION		
Fat (44% calories from fat) 27		g
Protein 23		g
Carbohydrate 56		g
Cholesterol 302		mg
Sodium 3		mg

Arugula-Filled Pockets

Elegant • For company

• For dough, mix flour with eggs, oil, about 6 tablespoons water, and 1 teaspoon salt. Knead to form smooth, elastic dough (see page 50). If dough is dry, knead in more water. If too sticky, knead in more flour. Cover dough with cloth and let rest at room temperature about 30 minutes.

• For filling, trim arugula and chop finely. Trim leek, halve lengthwise, and wash thoroughly. Finely chop white and bright green parts. Mince onions. Finely chop parsley leaves. Mix vegetables with 1 teaspoon salt and let stand 10 minutes. Place in sieve and press out all liquid.

• Dice toast and soak in milk. Press out all milk. Add bread, egg, and egg yolk to arugula mixture to make thick filling. Season well with salt, pepper, and nutmeg.

• Cut dough into 3 pieces. Roll out on lightly floured surface until paper thin. Cut dough into pieces 2½ × 5 inches (6 × 12 cm). Mound 1 level tablespoon arugula filling in center of each piece. Brush edges with water, fold over, and press edges firmly together.

• Using 1 large pot or 2 small ones, bring vegetable broth to boil. Boil pockets 10 minutes.

• Core tomatoes and cut into small cubes. Finely chop parsley leaves and mix with tomato cubes. Melt butter in pan. Add tomato mixture and sauté over medium heat 2 to 3 minutes.

• Drain pockets and place in warm bowls. Ladle some broth over pockets. Serve garnished with tomato mixture.

Makes 4 to 6 servings

For Dough:

2 cups (300 g) semolina or spelt flour (sold in health food stores)
2 eggs
1 tablespoon vegetable oil
Salt
Flour for work surface

For Filling:

1 lb (400 g) arugula
1 leek (about 5 oz/150 g)
2 onions
1 bunch parsley
Salt
4 slices white bread, toasted
1 scant cup (200 ml) milk
1 egg
1 egg yolk
Black pepper
Freshly grated nutmeg
2 qts (2 l) vegetable broth
3 tomatoes
½ bunch parsley
2 tablespoons butter

Preparation time: about 2 hours

PER SERVING:	390 CALORIES
NUTRITIONAL INFORMATION	
Fat (31% calories from fat) . . . . 13 g	
Protein . . . . 15 g	
Carbohydrate . . . . 51 g	
Cholesterol . . . . 222 mg	
Sodium . . . . 2258 mg	

Feta Pockets with Yogurt Sauce

Economical • Time consuming

• Mix flour with 3 tablespoons oil, egg yolk, 1 teaspoon salt, and lukewarm water. Knead to form smooth, elastic dough (see page 50). Shape dough into ball, cover with damp cloth, and let rest at room temperature about 30 minutes.

• Finely mash feta with fork. Mince onions and garlic. Tear off parsley leaves and chop finely.

• Mix cheese with onion mixture, parsley, and egg. Season with paprika. You probably will not need salt, as cheese is already well salted.

• Knead dough again. Roll out on lightly floured surface until paper thin, then make dough even thinner by stretching with backs of hands. Cut sheet of dough into 6×4-inch (15×10 cm) rectangles. Mound filling at one side, leaving edges clear. Brush edges with water, fold over, and press edges firmly together.

• For sauce, finely chop mint leaves. Beat yogurt with mineral water until creamy. Stir in mint and season with salt and cumin.

• Heat 2 tablespoons oil in each of 2 skillets. Sauté pockets over medium heat 4 minutes on each side or until crisp and brown. Serve with cold yogurt sauce.

Makes 4 servings.

Tip:

Zucchini slices sautéed in olive oil until golden and sprinkled with slivered lemon peel are excellent with this dish.

For Pockets:
1⅔ cups (250 g) all-purpose flour
Vegetable oil
1 egg yolk
Salt
½ cup (100 ml) lukewarm water
Flour for work surface

For Filling:
12 oz (300 g) feta cheese
2 red onions
2 garlic cloves
2 large bunches parsley
1 egg
1 teaspoon hot paprika
Few sprigs fresh mint
1 cup (250 g) plain yogurt
½ cup carbonated mineral water
Pinch of ground cumin

Preparation time: about 1½ hours

PER SERVING:	593 CALORIES
NUTRITIONAL INFORMATION	
Fat (46% calories from fat) . . . . .30 g	
Protein . . . . .26 g	
Carbohydrate .55 g	
Cholesterol . . . . .193 mg	
Sodium . . . . .3 mg	

Steamed Dumplings with Vegetable Nut Filling

From China • Easy to prepare

- For dumplings, mix flour, 1 teaspoon salt, and water and knead until smooth and elastic (see page 50). Cover dough with damp cloth and let rest at room temperature about 30 minutes.

- For filling, soak mushrooms in lukewarm water about 30 minutes. Drain, remove hard stems, and mince caps. Finely grate carrot. Clean pepper halves and chop finely. Trim leek, wash, and mince, including tender green parts. Mince garlic. Finely chop peanuts. Tear off cilantro leaves and chop finely.

- Mix mushrooms with vegetables, garlic, peanuts, and cilantro. Season with soy sauce and chili oil. Mix egg whites and cornstarch. Stir into vegetable mixture.

- Knead dough again and roll out on lightly floured surface until paper thin. Using glass or cookie cutter, cut into 3-in (8 cm) rounds. Mound filling in center. Brush edges of dough with water. Gather up edges of round and pinch together firmly above filling.

- For sauce, peel ginger and grate finely. Peel cucumber and halve lengthwise; scoop out and discard seeds. Mince cucumber. Mix soy sauce with vinegar, peanut butter, chili oil, and 6 tablespoons water until well blended. Stir in ginger and cucumber.

- Place dumplings side by side on lightly oiled perforated steam basket or pan. Place over simmering water. Cover and steam about 10 minutes. Serve hot with cold sauce.

Makes 4 servings.

Tips:

If there is not enough room in the steamer to hold all the dumplings at the same time, steam them in batches, keeping cooked dumplings in a warm (200°F/50°C) oven. You can also use two steamers at once to make sure each batch is freshly cooked.
Tie each dumpling with a long strip of green onion for a decorative touch.

PER SERVING:	375 CALORIES
NUTRITIONAL INFORMATION	

Fat (22% calories from fat) 9	g
Protein 16	g
Carbohydrate 57	g
Cholesterol 0	mg
Sodium 1293	mg

For Dumplings:
1⅔ cups (250 g) all-purpose flour
Salt
½ cup (125 ml) cold water
Flour for work surface

For Filling:
10 dried shiitake mushrooms
1 carrot
½ green bell pepper
½ red bell pepper
1 leek
2 garlic cloves
2 oz (50 g) salted peanuts
Few sprigs fresh cilantro (coriander)
2 tablespoons soy sauce
Few drops chili oil
2 egg whites
2 teaspoons cornstarch

For Sauce:
1 oz (30 g) fresh ginger root
1 small cucumber
¼ cup (60 ml) soy sauce
1½ teaspoons rice vinegar
2 teaspoons peanut butter
1 teaspoon chili oil

Preparation time: about 1 hour and 10 minutes

77

Crunch, crunch...

From the Oven

What is more tempting than a fragrant, appetizing, golden-crusted baked noodle dish? It's the perfect dish for company, for once the mixture is prepared and in the oven, there is nothing left to do but greet the guests and enjoy the evening.

The Correct Noodle

Certain noodle varieties are better than others for these savory, crusty baked dishes.

Cannelloni tubes and lasagne noodles are the classics. Both are available made with whole-grain flour or colored green with spinach. Some cannelloni and lasagne noodles must be precooked before filling, and some can be used without precooking.

When lasagne and cannelloni are prepared without precooking, the filling must be moist, because the noodles will absorb more liquid as they cook.

For soufflés and gratins, it is best to use short noodles; they are easier to fold into the other ingredients.

Spaghetti or fine noodles can be shaped into small nests with a fork after cooking and draining. Place nests side by side on a greased baking sheet. Top with cooked vegetables and grated cheese. Bake at 325°F (160°C) only until cheese melts and is golden brown.

The Best Melting Cheese

Cheese gives the oven dish its appetizing crust and unique taste. It is most important to choose a cheese that melts quickly and smoothly.

The best choices are aromatic hard cheeses such as Emmentaler (Swiss), Gruyère, Appenzeller, and aged Gouda. Next best are aged pecorino or Spanish Manchego. Blue-veined cheeses such as Gorgonzola and Roquefort have a wonderful aroma. For delicate and creamy dishes, it's better to use mozzarella, preferably made from buffalo milk, which is creamier and more delicate than one made from cow's milk. It's easy to purchase in many supermarkets and cheese shops.

Parmesan mixes best into a soufflé or gratin. By itself, though, Parmesan is not good for sprinkling on top, as it hardens when baked. Therefore, dot Parmesan with pieces of butter or drizzle with oil before baking.

The Correct Baking Dish

For plenty of crust, bake the mixture in a large, flat baking dish. If you want the dish to be moist and not so crisp, choose a smaller, deeper baking dish. For lasagne and cannelloni, use square or oblong baking dishes suitable for the shape and size of the noodle. And choose a good-looking dish that can go right from oven to table.

Whole-Grain or Not

Many of the most nutritious noodles have a strong taste of whole grains, which you may or may not like. Make the effort to taste several brands of whole-grain noodles to find a brand that tastes good and harmonizes with delicate sauces. In Italy, whole-grain pastas can be found in every supermarket, and they taste terrific. Look for imports in supermarkets, specialty shops, and health food stores.

Bechamel Sauce with Variations

Almost any vegetable can be used in a simple yet tasty lasagne made with bechamel sauce and uncooked lasagne noodles layered in a baking dish. Use vegetables raw (bell peppers, peas, carrots, zucchini, and kohlrabi in very thin slices), sautéed (mushrooms, eggplant), or blanched (spinach, beet greens, asparagus, sugar snap peas, or snow peas). For the bechamel, melt 2 oz (1/2 stick/60 g) butter in saucepan. Add 1/3 cup (50 to 60 g) all-purpose or whole-grain flour. Stir over low heat until golden brown.

Gradually add 1 qt (1 l) milk, stirring constantly over low heat until well blended. Simmer, stirring, 10 minutes. Season sauce with salt, pepper, and nutmeg. If desired, stir in 2 to 2 1/2 oz (50 to 75 g) freshly grated Parmesan or pecorino.

2½ lbs (1 kg) fennel bulbs
Salt
2 teaspoons fennel seeds
1 lemon
1 bunch fresh dill
2 garlic cloves
2 beefsteak tomatoes
10 oz (300 g) Gorgonzola
1 scant cup (200 ml) heavy
cream
1 scant cup (200 ml) milk
2 oz (50 g) Parmesan,
freshly grated
Black pepper
9 oz (250 g) lasagne noodles
(no precooking needed)
5 oz (125 g) mozzarella

Preparation time: about
1½ hours (includes 40
minutes baking time)

Lasagne with Fennel and Gorgonzola
Easy • For company

• Trim fennel. Halve lengthwise and cut out cores. Blanch fennel in boiling salted water about 4 minutes. Rinse with cold water, drain, and cut into thin crosswise slices. Set aside delicate fennel greens.

• Crush fennel seeds in mortar. Thinly slice off lemon peel and mince. Press juice from lemon half. Cut off feathery tips of dill. Mince garlic. Core tomatoes, dip into boiling water, peel, halve, and dice finely.

• Mash Gorgonzola and beat with cream and milk until smooth. Stir in Parmesan and lemon juice. Season with salt and pepper.

• Preheat oven to 350°F (180°C). Mix fennel with lemon peel, garlic, dill, and fennel seeds and season with salt and pepper. Line greased rectangular baking dish with layer of uncooked lasagne noodles. Add layer of fennel mixture and half of tomatoes. Add layer of cheese mixture.

• Continue layering; top layer should be noodles covered with cheese mixture and sprinkled with tomato. Cut mozzarella into cubes and sprinkle over top.

• Bake lasagne in center of oven about 40 minutes or until noodles are tender and top is golden brown. Finely chop reserved fennel greens and sprinkle over lasagne.

Makes 4 servings.

Variation:
Instead of fennel, use blanched beet greens or savoy cabbage leaves. Oyster mushrooms, cut into strips and sautéed in olive oil until golden, can be layered with the other ingredients.

PER SERVING:	916 CALORIES	
NUTRITIONAL INFORMATION		
Fat (44% calories from fat)	50	g
Protein	83	g
Carbohydrate	63	g
Cholesterol	63	mg
Sodium	14	mg

*2¼ lbs (1 kg) pumpkin
(trimmed weight 1½ lbs/
750 g)
Salt
1 bunch green onions
2 garlic cloves
2 bunches fresh basil
2 oz (50 g) blanched
almonds
2 tablespoons capers
3 oz (80 g) black olives
4 oz (125 g) mozzarella
⅔ cup (150 ml) crème
fraîche (or ½ cup/125 ml
heavy cream and ¼ cup/
60 ml sour cream)
5 oz (150 g) pecorino, freshly
grated
Black pepper
Cayenne pepper
1 lb (400 g) tomatoes
2 tablespoons olive oil
9 oz (250 g) cannelloni tubes
(no precooking needed)*

*Preparation time: about
1¼ hours (includes 40
minutes baking time)*

Cannelloni with Pumpkin and Olives

Elegant • Autumn Dish

• Peel pumpkin; remove seeds and strings. Dice pumpkin. Bring salted water to boil in a pot and boil pumpkin until tender, about 5 minutes. Rinse with cold water and drain. Coarsely chop pumpkin in food processor.

• Trim green onions, wash thoroughly and cut into thin rings with tender green parts. Peel garlic and force through garlic press. Cut basil leaves into strips. Finely chop almonds and toast in dry pan over medium heat, stirring, until golden. Drain capers and mince. Pit olives and cut into strips. Cut mozzarella into small cubes.

• Mix pumpkin, green onions, garlic, basil, almonds, capers, and olives with crème fraîche and 1 cup (100 g) of the grated pecorino. Stir in mozzarella and season with salt, pepper, and cayenne.

• Core tomatoes. Dip into boiling water, peel, and cut into small cubes. Sprinkle with salt and 1 tablespoon olive oil.

• Preheat oven to 350°F (180°C). Stuff uncooked cannelloni with pumpkin mixture (this is easier to do using pastry bag without a tip). Place tubes side by side in greased large baking dish. Spoon tomato mixture over top and sprinkle with remaining pecorino. Drizzle with remaining oil.

• Bake cannelloni about 40 minutes or until pasta is tender and top is golden brown.

Makes 4 servings.

Tip:

For a quicker dish, substitute canned peeled whole tomatoes, finely diced, for the fresh tomatoes.

PER SERVING:	780 CALORIES
NUTRITIONAL INFORMATION	

Fat (52% calories from fat) 45		g
Protein 30		g
Carbohydrate 64		g
Cholesterol 66		mg
Sodium 227		mg

Penne Eggplant Gratin
Salt
10 oz (300 g) penne
10 oz (300 g) tomatoes
2 small eggplants (about
1 lb/500 g)
3 to 4 sprigs mint
1 red chili pepper (optional)
2 garlic cloves
4 to 5 tablespoons olive oil
Pepper
Cayenne pepper
9 oz (250 g) feta cheese
⅔ cup (150 ml) plain yogurt
8 to 12 black olives

Preparation time: about
1¼ hours (includes 35
minutes baking time)

Green Noodles au Gratin
12 green lasagne noodles
Salt
About 20 savoy cabbage
leaves or beet greens
1 sprig fresh tarragon
2 tomatoes
1 lb (400 g) cream cheese,
Neufchatel, or mascarpone
2 eggs
5 oz (150 g) pecorino, freshly
grated
2 tablespoons sunflower
seeds
Black pepper
Cayenne pepper
4 tablespoons olive oil (or
more if needed)

Preparation time: about
50 minutes

Penne Eggplant Gratin

Light • Easy to prepare

• Boil penne in salted water until al dente. Rinse with cold water and drain.

• Dip tomatoes into boiling water, peel, and cut into small cubes. Trim eggplant and dice. Finely chop mint leaves. Trim and mince chili pepper. Mince garlic.

• Preheat oven to 400°F (200°C). Heat 2 tablespoons oil in large skillet and sauté eggplant in batches until golden, adding more oil as necessary. Sauté garlic and chili pepper briefly. In bowl, mix eggplant, garlic, chili pepper, penne, tomatoes, and mint. Season with salt, pepper, and cayenne.

• Mash feta and mix with yogurt. Season with pepper. Spoon penne mixture into greased baking dish and top with feta mixture. Sprinkle with olives. Bake 35 minutes.

Makes 4 servings.

PER SERVING:	581 CALORIES	
NUTRITIONAL INFORMATION		
Fat (38% calories from fat)	24	g
Protein	25	g
Carbohydrate	64	g
Cholesterol	28	mg
Sodium	128	mg

Green Noodles au Gratin

Pictured • Easy to prepare

• Cook noodles in boiling salted water 2 to 3 minutes or until softened. Rinse with cold water and leave in water.

• Carefully remove cabbage leaves and cut ribs flat. Blanch in boiling salted water 2 to 3 minutes. Rinse with cold water and drain. Cut cabbage into pieces that fit on lasagne noodles. Finely chop tarragon leaves. Core and dice tomatoes. Mash cream cheese until soft. Mix with tarragon, tomatoes, eggs, half the pecorino, and sunflower seeds. Season with salt, pepper, and cayenne.

• Preheat oven to 400°F (200°C). Drain noodles well. Spread cheese mixture on cabbage leaves. Place on noodles. Roll noodles up loosely and place rolls side by side in greased baking dish. Sprinkle with remaining pecorino. Drizzle with oil. Bake uncovered 10 minutes. Cover and bake an additional 15 minutes.

Makes 4 servings.

PER SERVING:	811 CALORIES	
NUTRITIONAL INFORMATION		
Fat (59% calories from fat)	53	g
Protein	27	g
Carbohydrate	57	g
Cholesterol	258	mg
Sodium	29	mg

Penne au Gratin with Vegetable Balls

Elegant • Economical

• For penne, bring plenty of water to boil. Add salt and penne and boil until al dente. Rinse with cold water and drain.

• Core tomatoes and dip in boiling water. Peel and cut into small cubes. Cut basil leaves into strips. Peel garlic and force through garlic press.

• Mix penne with tomatoes, basil, garlic, and crème fraîche. Season with salt, pepper, and cayenne.

• Trim broccoli and cut into florets, discarding hard stems. Peel and dice carrots. Cook broccoli and carrots in salted boiling water 6 to 8 minutes or until very tender. Rinse with cold water and drain. Puree broccoli and carrots separately in food processor.

• Finely chop parsley leaves. Mix mascarpone with egg yolks and pecorino. Mix half of cheese mixture with carrot puree, parsley, and tomato paste. Season with salt and pepper.

• Mix remaining cheese mixture with broccoli puree, almonds, and grated lemon peel. Season with salt and pepper.

• Preheat oven to 350°F (180°C). Spread penne mixture in greased baking dish. With wet spoon, scoop egg-shaped mounds of broccoli mixture alternating with mounds of carrot mixture side by side on top of noodles. Dot top with butter and bake 35 minutes or until penne and vegetable balls are golden brown.

Makes 4 servings.

Salt
8 oz (200 g) penne (or ziti)
1 lb (400 g) tomatoes
1 bunch fresh basil
2 garlic cloves
¼ cup (60 ml) crème fraîche or sour cream
Black pepper
Cayenne pepper
8 oz (250 g) broccoli
8 oz (250 g) carrots
1 bunch parsley
8 oz (250 g) mascarpone
2 egg yolks
4 oz (100 g) pecorino or Parmesan, freshly grated
1 tablespoon tomato paste
1 tablespoon grated almonds
1 teaspoon grated lemon peel
1 tablespoon butter

Preparation time: about 1¼ hours (includes 35 minutes baking time)

PER SERVING:	743 CALORIES
NUTRITIONAL INFORMATION	
Fat (60% calories from fat) 49	g
Protein 25	g
Carbohydrate 49	g
Cholesterol 280	mg
Sodium 45	mg

1 lb (450 g) sauerkraut
1 onion
1 tablespoon vegetable oil
1 cup (200 ml) vegetable
broth or sauerkraut juice
Salt
8 oz (250 g) large pasta
shells (conchiglione)
1 small green apple
1 red bell pepper
4 oz (125 g) mozzarella
1 tablespoon chopped
walnuts
2 oz (50 g) Swiss cheese,
freshly grated
1 egg
1 scant cup (200 ml) heavy
cream or crème fraîche
Black pepper
1 teaspoon hot paprika
1 bunch green onions
2 tablespoons butter

*Preparation time: 1¼ to 1½
hours (includes 25 to 30
minutes baking time)*

Conchiglione with Sauerkraut Filling

Elegant • Easy to prepare

• Drain sauerkraut and chop finely. Mince onion. Heat oil in pot and sauté onion until translucent. Add sauerkraut and sauté another few minutes. Add broth, cover, and simmer over medium heat about 20 minutes. Let cool.

• Bring plenty of water to boil. Add salt and pasta shells and boil about 13 minutes or until al dente. Rinse with cold water and drain.

• Peel, quarter, and core apple. Cut into thin slices. Halve pepper, remove seeds, and cut into small cubes. Drain mozzarella and cut into small cubes.

• Mix sauerkraut with apple, pepper, mozzarella, walnuts, Swiss cheese, egg, and cream. Season with salt, pepper, and paprika.

• Trim green onions and cut into thin rings with tender green parts.

• Preheat oven to 400°F (200°C). Spoon sauerkraut mixture into pasta shells. Place side by side in greased baking dish. Sprinkle with green onions. Dot with butter.

• Bake 25 to 30 minutes or until golden brown.

Makes 4 servings.

Variation:
Spinach Nut Filling
Blanch 1½ lbs (600 g) fresh spinach in boiling water until wilted. Rinse with cold water and squeeze as dry as possible. Chop finely. Sauté 2 finely chopped shallots in 1 tablespoon butter until golden. Mix spinach with shallots, 3 tablespoons crème fraîche or sour cream, 4 oz (100 g) chopped walnuts, 1¾ cups (200 g) freshly grated Swiss cheese, 1 egg, salt, pepper, and nutmeg. Fill cooked pasta shells with mixture. Place side by side in greased baking dish. Pour over ½ cup (125 ml) heavy cream and bake as above.

PER SERVING:	687 CALORIES
NUTRITIONAL INFORMATION	
Fat (46% calories from fat) 35	g
Protein 26	g
Carbohydrate 67	g
Cholesterol 142	mg
Sodium 355	mg

Fusilli Soufflé with Mushrooms

9 oz (250 g) fusilli
Salt
1 lb (400 g) wild mushrooms
2 tablespoons butter
Black pepper
1 bunch mixed herbs
1 bunch arugula
1 bunch green onions
½ lemon
3 eggs
½ cup (100 g) ricotta
½ cup (125 ml) milk
3 oz (80 g) pecorino or
Parmesan, freshly grated

Preparation time: about
1 hour and 20 minutes
(includes 35 minutes
baking time)

Noodle Soufflé with Smoked Tofu

8 oz (200 g) medium white
or green noodles
Salt
1 lb (500 g) Brussels sprouts
8 oz (200 g) smoked tofu
(with mushrooms, if
available)
1 bunch parsley
Black pepper
Freshly grated nutmeg
4 eggs
1 scant cup (200 ml) heavy
cream
4 oz (100 g) Swiss cheese,
freshly grated

Preparation time: about
1 hour and 10 minutes
(includes 30 minutes
baking time)

Fusilli Soufflé with Mushrooms

Light • Easy to prepare

• Cook fusilli in boiling salted water until al dente. Rinse with cold water and drain.

• Clean mushrooms and cut into thin slices. Heat 1 tablespoon butter and sauté mushrooms until golden brown. Season with salt and pepper.

• Trim herbs and arugula and chop finely. Trim green onions and cut into thin rings. Thinly slice off lemon peel and mince. Juice lemon.

• Preheat oven to 400°F (200°C). Separate eggs. Mix yolks with ricotta, milk, lemon juice, and pecorino. Stir in fusilli, mushrooms, herbs, green onions, and lemon peel. Beat egg whites until stiff and fold into fusilli mixture. Pour into greased baking dish. Dot top with remaining butter. Bake about 35 minutes or until puffed and golden.

Makes 4 servings.

PER SERVING:	515 CALORIES	
NUTRITIONAL INFORMATION		
Fat (36% calories from fat) 21		g
Protein 27		g
Carbohydrate 57		g
Cholesterol 276		mg
Sodium 40		mg

Noodle Soufflé with Smoked Tofu

Pictured • Light

• Cook noodles in boiling salted water until al dente. Rinse with cold water and drain.

• Trim Brussels sprouts and blanch in boiling water 3 to 4 minutes. Rinse with cold water, drain, and cut into thin slices. Dice tofu. Tear off parsley leaves. Set aside a few leaves for garnish and chop remaining parsley.

• Mix noodles with Brussels sprouts, tofu, and chopped parsley. Season with salt, pepper, and nutmeg. Preheat oven to 400°F (200°C).

• Separate eggs. Mix yolks with cream and 3 oz (70 g) of the cheese. Fold in noodle mixture. Beat egg whites until stiff. Fold into noodle mixture. Pour into greased baking dish and sprinkle with remaining cheese.

• Bake about 30 minutes or until puffed and golden.

Makes 4 servings.

PER SERVING:	609 CALORIES	
NUTRITIONAL INFORMATION		
Fat (51% calories from fat) 34		g
Protein 30		g
Carbohydrate 44		g
Cholesterol 388		mg
Sodium 47		mg

INDEX

Published originally under the title *NUDELN—VEGETARISCH DURCH DIE PASTAWELT.*
© 1998 by Gräfe und Unzer Verlag GmbH, Munchen
English translation © Copyright 1999 by Barron's Educational Series, Inc.
German edition by Cornelia Schinharl
Photography by Heinz-Josef Beckers
English translation by Helen Feingold

All inquiries should be addressed to:
Barron's Educational Series, Inc.
250 Wireless Boulevard
Hauppauge, NY 11788
http://www.barronseduc.com

Library of Congress Catalog Card No. 99-31700

International Standard Book No. 0-7641-1278-3

Library of Congress Cataloging-in-Publication Data

Schinharl, Cornelia.
    [Nudeln. English]
    Noodles : a vegetarian journey
        through the world of pasta /
    Cornelia Schinharl ; photography
    by Heinz-Josef Beckers ; translated
    from the German by Helen
    Feingold.
        p.   cm.
    Includes index.
    ISBN 0-7641-1278-3
    1. Cookery (Pasta) 2.
    Vegetarian cookery. 3. Noodles.
    I. Title.
    TX809.M17S246   2000   99-31700
                                CIP

Printed in Hong Kong
9 8 7 6 5 4 3 2 1

Cornelia Schinharl lives in the vicinity of Munich, Germany and studied languages before she turned to the subject of food. She has always had a great interest in culinary subjects. After training with a well-known food journalist, and an internship in a large Hamburg, Germany publishing house, she became a free-lance editor and author in 1995. Since then, she has authored numerous books.

Heinz-Josef Beckers studied communications design at the University of Essen GHS (Folkwang). He maintains a studio for photography and design in the vicinity of Frankfurt am Main. Food, still lifes, and experimental photography are among his areas of specialization, along with conceptual and graphic work for industry, publishers, and agencies.

Kitchen Appliances and Helpful Hints

Spaetzle Grater

Choose between a spaetzle press and a spaetzle grater. The press is similar to a potato ricer. For long, thick spaetzle, place the dough in the hopper of the press, hold it over simmering salted water, and press the plunger to extrude the dough through the holes in the hopper. When a spaetzle grater (similar to a food mill) is used, the spaetzle will be short due to the rotation of the grater.

If these appliances are not available, place dough on a board. With the blade of a long knife that is dipped repeatedly in lukewarm water, scrape thin strips of dough off the board into simmering salted water. This takes more time but is easy to do.

Spaghetti Tongs

A dinner fork is the wrong tool to use for serving noodles covered with sauce. Spaghetti tongs hold tight and prevent slipping. They are available in chrome, stainless steel, plastic, or wood.

When testing the doneness of a noodle, use a spaghetti spoon with wooden pegs on one side to lift it from the boiling water.